Business Basics for Private Practice

Business Basics for Private Practice is a step-by-step guide to developing a successful practice from initial conceptualization and business plan to future growth for the true entrepreneur. Dr. Bartolucci draws from interviews with fellow mental health practitioners and experts in business-related fields to make even the most intimidating parts of practice easy to understand. *Business Basics* is written to give the feel of mentorship, and the author talks about lessons learned the hard way. She's also included checklists and worksheets to help you stay organized and ready to meet the challenges of opening a private practice.

Anne D. Bartolucci, PhD, CBSM, started her private practice in 2008 and has since become Atlanta's insomnia expert. She is also a sought-after speaker and business consultant.

Business Basics for Private Practice

A Guide for Mental Health Professionals

ANNE D. BARTOLUCCI

Routledge
Taylor & Francis Group

NEW YORK AND LONDON

First published 2018
by Routledge
711 Third Avenue, New York, NY 10017

and by Routledge
2 Park Square, Milton Park, Abingdon, Oxon, OX14 4RN

Routledge is an imprint of the Taylor & Francis Group, an informa business

Library of Congress Cataloging-in-Publication Data
Names: Bartolucci, Anne D., author.
Title: Business basics for private practice: a guide for mental health
professionals / by Anne D. Bartolucci.
Description: New York: Routledge, 2018. | Includes bibliographical
references.
Identifiers: LCCN 2017009906| ISBN 9781138690950 (hardback) |
ISBN 9781138690967 (pbk.) | ISBN 9781315472058 (eBook)
Subjects: | MESH: Office Management–organization & administration |
Private Practice | Mental Health Services–organization & administration
Classification: LCC RC465.5 | NLM W 80 | DDC 616.890068–dc23
LC record available at https://lccn.loc.gov/2017009906

ISBN: 978-1-138-69095-0 (hbk)
ISBN: 978-1-138-69096-7 (pbk)
ISBN: 978-1-315-47205-8 (ebk)

Typeset in Avenir and Dante
by Deanta Global Publishing Services, Chennai, India

This book is dedicated to all those who are brave enough to think beyond what they've been taught, foolish enough to take risks, and wise enough to know when to seek guidance. I'd also like to dedicate this book to my husband Jason, who's been my biggest supporter from the beginning of my practice.

Contents

List of Tables

Acknowledgments

Sometimes I get myself in trouble with an attitude of "let's see if I can do this" without considering what will happen if I succeed. When I was at the Association for Cognitive and Behavioral Therapies in Chicago in the autumn of 2015, I went looking for a book like this one. I asked the nice young lady at the Routledge booth if they had anything like this. That nice young lady turned out to be editor Anna Moore, and she said they didn't have a book like I was asking for, but she'd be interested in acquiring one. My overachiever personality went into overdrive, and so I put together a proposal. She accepted it, and I signed the contract with Routledge in February.

Anna is the first person I would like to thank. She knew I write fiction, but she took the chance on contracting me for something beyond what I'd ever attempted. I'd also like to thank her staff Dylan Ford and Nina Guttapalle.

Once I signed the contract, I wasn't prepared for how it came along with a major case of impostor syndrome. Unlike writing my novels, where I get to make up stuff and the only people involved are me and my characters, this book turned into a cooperative effort. It was anxiety-provoking since I was asking other professionals to give me their time and knowledge for very little in return. It was also encouraging because everyone I approached, but one, gave me a positive response. Every interview I did in person, by phone, or by email and every bit of feedback I received in the later stages of writing this book kept me enthusiastic about the process and helped me feel that I was on the right track and did have something to offer.

First, I'd like to specifically acknowledge and thank my amazing content readers. I originally called them beta readers, but the draft I gave them wasn't nearly polished enough to be called anything but a very preliminary first draft. Maggie Worth, coach, freelance writer, and owner of Wheat Germ, LLC, has the most amazing detail-oriented mind of anyone I've ever met. She helped me fill in holes in the manuscript that I had no idea were there, and she's not even a psychologist, although we do share a love of the Myers Briggs Type Indicator (MBTI) and personality theory. I also need to thank my two guinea pigs, Jackie Kloss, Clinical Associate Professor at the Drexel University College of Medicine, and Shelby Harris, Director of the Behavioral Sleep Medicine Program at the Sleep-Wake Disorders Center at Montefiore Medical Center and associate faculty at the Albert Einstein College of Medicine (psychiatry and neurology). I met both of them through our behavioral sleep medicine society and am honored to call them both colleagues and friends.

Second, I'm indebted to the professionals who helped me with my "Interview with the Expert" boxes. While real estate broker Weslee Knapp and I don't often cross paths, I always enjoy it when we do, and I was happy for the excuse to be back in touch with him. My connection with Linda Collett came through the Atlanta Independent Women's Network (AIWN), for whom both of us spoke on separate occasions last year. Her specialty is writing legal documents that we mere mortals can understand, and I appreciate her doing the same for the legal concepts in my interview with her. Donna Grindle of Kardon Compliance is another AIWN member. Although Kardon is based in Atlanta, they help practices all over the country, and they keep me compliant. I'm also grateful to Kelly Locklear of Small Business Solutions and Carly Berg of Above & Beyond Bookkeeping for their help with demystifying numbers.

I definitely want to give a special shout-out to Tyra Burton, senior lecturer at Kennesaw State University, for her help with the marketing chapter. She's the one that those of us in the Georgia Romance Writers go to when we have any questions about social media and websites. And I'd also like to thank Eric Marine of the American Professional Agency for sharing his knowledge and being so entertaining while he did so. I admit, I'd been dreading contacting the insurance guy, but his was one of the conversations I enjoyed the most.

Third, I can't express enough appreciation to my colleagues, who were kind enough to sit down with me in person, to take the time to chat by telephone, or to answer my emails. They're listed in the bibliographies, and I encourage you to check out their websites because you know they're doing something right. I'd especially like to thank Daniel Wachtel, Psy.D., who was my first interviewee and therefore helped me refine my questions and figure out how to ask exactly what I needed. The other psychologists who graciously shared their time, experience, and knowledge with me include Aynsley Corbett, Psy.D.; Debra Dantzler, PhD, LPC; Robin Day, LPC; Bill Herring, LCSW; Julie Kolzet, PhD; Pegah Moghaddam, Psy.D.; Shala Nicely, LPC; Katie Spencer, Psy.D.; and Josh Spitalnick, PhD, ABPP. I am indebted to all of you.

Then there are the behind-the-scenes people I need to thank. As I mentioned, Maggie Worth helped me in many places beyond where she's quoted. Gary Parnaby, Jr., a Marketing and Investment Associate at Merrill Lynch, was kind enough to look over my chapters on business structure and money and give valuable feedback. Like Maggie, he filled in holes I didn't know were there.

Much of what I learned in this practice came from my early business mentors, particularly Rebecca Beaton, PhD, of the Anxiety and Stress Management Institute, and Joni Prince, PhD, of Atlanta Psych Consultants. I'm grateful to have had their support and guidance in my early practice career. I'd also like to thank Ryan Wetzler, Psy.D., C.B.S.M. for his guidance in setting up a behavioral sleep medicine practice.

Last, but certainly not least, I have to thank my husband Jason. He supported me and encouraged me back in 2008 when I started my practice and kept me from freaking out when the economy tanked a month later. He kept me from exploding when Medicare returned my application three times. More recently, he pushed me along through that early impostor syndrome period with nudges to work on "that book you have a contract for." He was very sweet and patient toward the end of this process, when I locked myself away to work on the book for hours on end and/or was on the phone or computer doing interviews. He took up the bulk of the cooking the last week before deadline, and for that and many other signs of love and support, I can't thank him enough. There's a saying that behind every successful man is a strong woman. In my case, that works both ways.

Introduction

A Warning

I remember my hardest day in my practice so far. It was a lovely spring day outside, but inside, I was struggling. I had just gotten off the telephone with the telecommunications company I had just dumped a few months previously. Like a persistent ex, they couldn't accept that I wanted them to discontinue service on the one line I never used and therefore hadn't ported out. They refused to admit they had made a mistake, which ended up being a costly mistake for me. I was behind on records requests for patients who were applying for disability or who needed updated records for continuation, and a stack of messages sat on my desk, unanswered, since I'd had to deal with the telecommunications company and spent all the time on hold. Oh, and I was also seeing a full schedule of patients with all the inherent stressors of clinical work and was dealing with a strange and annoying high-pitched noise in one of the air vents in my ceiling that wouldn't stop no matter how many times the maintenance guy tried to fix it. Said air vent was directly over the chair I sat in while doing therapy, so it was hard to ignore, and I left work with a headache most days. They finally fixed it by replacing some of the duct work, but not for many months.

Running your own practice is not an easy task. If you're still reading, good for you. You may have the guts to do this.

When I decided to leave the security of a salaried position to start my own practice, I had very little inkling of how complicated it would be. I felt confident in my clinical skills and ability to interpret research, but as for running a business, I had no clue. One of the first lessons I learned is that time really is money, and the busier you are, the less you have to spare. I'm hoping with this book to save you time and money and to help you step into your practice with the groundwork laid and knowledge to do so more efficiently. Even if you do use this or another business book, I can't tell you how much it helps to have a business mentor, especially when you're starting out. I didn't realize how many questions I must have asked until I was in the position of mentor and wondering just how I could manage to maintain my own busy patient load, business responsibilities, and answer what felt like a thousand questions per day. I will always appreciate the guidance and encouragement I got from the doctors at the first practice I joined, which I'll talk about later. Another resource is the Small Business Administration, which has offices nationwide and offers free counseling and advice. When I started my practice, that's one of the first places I went.

Let's get back to you. Who is this book for?

- Anyone who is interested in being their own boss as long as they're fine with working harder for themselves than they ever have for someone else.
- Anyone who is wanting to open their own service-oriented practice and needs to know where to start.
- Anyone who is feeling overwhelmed by all the business stuff they didn't teach you in graduate school.

This book is aimed primarily at psychologists in private practice, but there's applicable information in here for other allied health professionals and medical professionals who don't need a large support staff or lots of fancy equipment. Or perhaps those who do have more need for equipment. They're all lines on the budget, after all.

When did you decide that private practice might be your desired career path? For me, it was the summer of 2008, when my contract with my first employer was up for renewal. It was a three-year contract, and I can't complain about the support they gave me during the first two years, when they paid for my licensure materials and process, and then when they supported me through my certification in behavioral sleep medicine. I learned a lot about general sleep medicine and how to interpret sleep studies, too, all of which gave me a very good skill set for a behavioral sleep medicine specialty niche. The problem was that I knew I would never be a partner in the practice—that honor was reserved for M.D.s only—and I also knew I was bringing home a mere fraction of what I made for the practice. The psychologist who had served as my post-doctoral supervisor had a space open in her practice, a group space-sharing arrangement. It was a big leap into the unknown, and what decided it for me was a gut feeling that if I let that opportunity pass, I would regret it. So, I turned in my notice at my original job and went out on my own. I supplemented my income as I started my practice by continuing to do sleep study interpretation for my original employer on a contract basis.

Writing this book has given me the opportunity to talk to other private practitioners across the country and the reasons for going into private practice are as varied as individuals themselves. It was very rare that someone told me they'd always wanted to do it and had it as a goal from before graduate school. Many of us come to it after starting our careers elsewhere and deciding we wanted more independence and control. Perhaps you're looking for a situation that will allow you more flexibility with regard to your time and work hours. Maybe you're in an academic job and would like to supplement your income with some private practice work on the side so you can start to transition out of having to chase grant money. Or you might have seen how well a certain treatment modality works and recognized there's a dearth of easily accessible practitioners who are experts in it. Whatever your reasons, and no matter whether you're starting full-time or part-time, I'm hoping to give you a realistic picture of what private practice is like and also share some of my own mistakes so you won't make them. I do recognize that my experience won't be yours, but as I've found in my interviews for this book, there are some aspects of practice that are universal no matter what part of the country you're in.

That brings up another caveat of this book—I'm writing for a United States audience, so I'm not sure how some of these principles will translate to Canada or other countries, particularly with regard to government regulations and healthcare structure. There are also regional differences in the U.S., for example, in insurance coverage, so I will talk about insurance generally and not mention any particular providers except Medicare. Plus, the insurance landscape is shifting and changing constantly, and this is a time of great flux.

This book won't provide all the answers you need, but if I don't have an answer to your particular question, I will try to give you additional resources for where to look. You'll also notice that I draw from sources outside the realm of psychology. I have a not-so-secret identity as a fiction writer, and I've gotten some valuable information about promotion through learning about how to market myself in that arena. I've handpicked the books that I've found to be the most useful for my practice and encourage you to check them out.

One other thing to remember is that you do have to have some business skills or at least a desire to learn them. Don't worry, it won't be like those graduate school statistics courses—the math is pretty basic, and there are programs to do most of it for you. The concepts are a little more difficult, but again, nothing worse than anything you did in your training. You may surprise yourself by liking the business aspects of practice even if you feel frightened of math. Personally, I find it very interesting to see where the money goes and how it flows in and out. Yes, budgeting sometimes feels like more of an art than a science, but I'm getting better at it. As for a business plan, I'll admit that I'm learning that one along with you in this book, mostly because I've had to change my practice structure as other parts of my life have changed.

That's another beauty of having your own practice—you can adjust your business model and workflow as life shifts and opportunities arise.

How to Use This Book

In this book, I've tried to present the information in the order that it's best to consider it. Some things will need to be addressed simultaneously. For example, there will be work on the front end before you open your doors to clients. Laying the groundwork may seem tedious, but it will save you a lot of headaches in the end.

The chapters will consist of the following parts:

- General Information.
- "Interviews with the Expert" boxes, where I've been able to find someone who has more information about this stuff than I do. There won't be one for every chapter, but I'm excited for the ones I do have.
- Anecdotes about mistakes I've made or challenges I've faced. You can laugh along with me—I'm perfectly okay with self-deprecation and mockery.
- Checklists (if applicable), example forms, and/or worksheets at the back of each chapter to help you think more deeply about the topic.

I hate it when books tell me how to read them, so the recommended order is just a suggestion. You may find that you've already done some of this stuff or that you have resources available to you, so you don't have to worry about some of the information. I still encourage you to read those sections to make sure you're not inadvertently leaving anything out. There are a lot of details.

Also, I've used the terms client and patient interchangeably. While I realize that most psychotherapists refer to the people who seek help from them professionally as "clients," I and others in health psychology-related fields refer to them as patients to keep the language consistent with referral sources, who are mostly physicians. I also use the terms psychologist, psychotherapist, therapist, and provider to refer to you and me. Using the same word throughout would be repetitive, and I do believe that elements of this book will be helpful to other allied health professionals and smaller healthcare practices. I'm aware that in some states, including mine, Master's-level providers can't use the term psychologist, so I've tried to minimize use of that and other restrictive terms, but it might slip through since that's how I refer to myself. Finally, to help maintain confidentiality, I've used the inclusive pronoun "them" in some places. I hope that won't offend any grammar sticklers, but at least it is allowed now.

Ready to get started? Grab your beverage of choice, a writing implement for the worksheets, and get ready for an adventure.

Thank you for allowing me to be your guide.

Nuts and Bolts

I

Planning for Success   1

I was recently at the American Academy of Sleep Medicine conference, where a colleague of mine was relating to me how he had moved to a new city in the Southwest because his wife had found a great job there. He'd found a position with another practice but once he arrived, he realized their expectations were not in line with his life / work balance values, so he decided to start his own private practice. The shocked expression on his face as he related how much he had to do before he even opened his doors mirrored my own, which I remember well. We may have been on opposite sides of the country, but our experiences were similar. This book is for people like him who need a step-by-step guide for what to do and when to do it.

In this chapter, we'll go through the initial decision-making process and talk about a step that a lot of psychologists—including myself, I'm ashamed to say—tend to skip: writing a business plan. While it can seem intimidating, it's a good place to practice switching between the therapist mindset and the businessperson mindset. In order to have a successful private practice, you need both, and it's useful to be able to shift between them as needed.

Types of Practice Structure

Television shows typically depict psychologists and other mental health professionals in their own space, sometimes with an administrator, but generally on their own. In the 1980s television show *Growing Pains*, the father character, Alan Seaver, was a psychiatrist with an in-home practice. Bob Newhart is another example from an even older era (sorry, Mom and Dad, he's not that ancient, really) and he, too, is shown in what we picture as a typical office structure and space for a solo practitioner. However, this is just one type of practice; you have many options. Each practice structure has its pros and cons, and the one you choose will depend on how much control you like over your environment and finances. That sounds ominous, doesn't it? Don't be frightened—there's a practice structure for every kind of personality. Although there are as many types of practice as there are people who have creative ways of putting them together, I'm going to focus on some of the main ones. This is by no means a comprehensive list, so if you do come up with a different type, please tell me! I'm always happy to learn.

The Solo Private Practice

In my previous practice, each morning when I came in, I would unlock the door to my office if my administrator hadn't beaten me to it (she typically did—at least one of us is a morning person), turn on the lights and white noise machines, and check messages. I'd look at my calendar, to see if there were any cancellations, and make adjustments. I'd log in to my insurance clearinghouse site, download Explanation of Benefits (EOBs), and enter payments in to my accounting software. If I had time, I'd pay bills, and if needed, order office supplies either then or at lunchtime.

Oh, wait, I still do most of that stuff, although I'm hoping to delegate some of it as the practice grows and it gets too overwhelming. But for now, I'm still essentially a solo practitioner, so the control—and responsibility—of the office is mine.

If you have a very independent streak and are considering private practice because you don't want to work for anyone else, or if you want as much control over your environment, business, and schedule as possible, solo independent private practice is for you. The main advantages are not having to answer to anyone, flexibility to try new things, and creating the environment according to your standards and preferences. This goes for the big things like paint colors to the small things like whether you have a water service or whether you have to haul 5-gallon plastic jugs to the office from the grocery store every week.

Yes, I used to do that. I don't anymore since I now have a water service.

One of the major disadvantages of solo private practice is that it can get lonely. I've found myself missing the collegiality of having another provider in the office, someone who speaks the same language of mental health, and the opportunity for on-the-fly consultation or commiseration, as the case warrants. If you'd prefer having someone more available to consult with and to share the financial and other responsibilities, consider looking into the next practice structure, space sharing.

Space Sharing

In a space sharing arrangement, the practitioners split the costs—rent, administrative, utilities (if applicable)—of a space while maintaining their own private practices. Sometimes they go under one umbrella name, whereas at other times they maintain their own practices and businesses.

When I started my private practice, I joined a group of psychologists and psychiatrists who shared space in a seven-office suite in a Class A (top tier of office space—see Chapter 3) building in an area called "Pill Hill," near three major hospitals and several medical offices. We were under the umbrella of the larger practice with our own cards from that business, but for tax purposes we were all incorporated separately and had our own businesses. We paid rent to the central practice, and in return got space, access to the copier, office supplies, and administrative help. Since I didn't have a book like this, it was really helpful to have other practitioners who had been through it all before to ask when I came up against a challenge with regard to business or patient matters.

Being in a group practice can facilitate the referral process. Not only do the practitioners within the group refer each other—for example, I used to get referrals from my colleagues for patients with sleep problems—but when someone called the practice who didn't have a specific doctor in mind, the office manager would match them up or assign them to the next doctor on the list. The flexibility in this arrangement allows for all sorts of interesting cross-referral combinations, for example, a psychologist with a dietitian or other compatible allied health professional. I'll talk more about this in Chapter 10.

A disadvantage of this type of arrangement is the lack of control over certain aspects of the business. For example, one tiny thing that bothered me was that I didn't like using yellow-lined pads for psychotherapy notes, but they wouldn't buy white ones for me. I had to get my own. Also, I knew I would eventually want to expand my business and take on other health psychologists, but I couldn't do it in that office because there simply wasn't enough space. After I left, the practice ended up having to move, and while I'm sure the two main partners asked for input, it's not something the others had planned for or might have wanted to do. I've also heard of other practices where providers were left having to scramble for space when the principal decided to retire.

Embedded Practice

In this case, the practitioner is housed in another larger practice but still maintains their own business. For example, many health psychologists are embedded in a medical practice. The major advantages of this type of arrangement are that the main practice can handle scheduling and possibly billing, and being in the space facilitates referrals, specifically the "soft handoff," where the medical or other main practice provider can walk the patient down to the practitioner's space and introduce them. This increases the chances of the patient following up with the practitioner.

The major disadvantages of embedded practice are limited office hours, unless other arrangements can be made, again lack of control over the environment, and the fact that if the medical practice is housed in a high-rent area, the practitioner has to pay commercial rates in order not to be in violation of the law. Then there is the share of the administrative costs and the other potential expenses that may not be included in the rent.

Partnership

I saved this type of private practice for last because I highly recommend that you engage in space sharing before committing to a business partnership. Going into business with someone is kind of like dating—you're typically not going to become engaged unless you really know them. One business mentor I know recommends working with someone for at least two years before offering them partnership, and I agree.

In a business partnership, you're both or all part-owners of the business, and you share the responsibilities, costs, and profits. This means that major decisions need to be undertaken and agreed upon by all involved. There's definitely a certain level of maturity required and respect for the needs of everyone, both personal and professional. Again, this is an area where I would recommend outside consultation and mentorship to make sure the business agreement, and contract arrived upon, is fair to everyone.

The Business Plan

When I first heard of the concept of a business plan, I was somewhat taken aback. Isn't the plan to make more money than you spend so you can pay yourself and your bills and save up for unexpected expenses and retirement?

The truth is, it's not that simple. Just as we need ways to measure our clients' progress, we need to have a map for how we'll know our business is successful and when it's time to change strategies.

Looking at other books on private practice, it's apparent that business plans, just like assessment instruments, can be as simple or as complicated as you'd like. I don't have much patience for paperwork, so my thought is that the simpler it is, the more likely it is you'll make one and keep up with reassessing it. There are many online classes and resources, free and paid, if you want more guidance with your plan. The Small Business Administration is also a great resource here.

One thing I've done that I found helpful was to take a course on strategic planning, which was aimed at writers. Strategic planning can apply to anyone, not just writers, and the most beneficial part was to help me define my mission statement for both my careers. When you're drafting your business plan, you might find it helpful to define your own mission statement and values as a guide before you start.

What is a mission statement? It's a statement of what you do and how you do it. Think first about how you want to make a change for your clients and in your community through your practice. Then find the part that you're passionate about and hone in on that. For example, my mission statement is to help my clients (and readers) see the world and themselves in a new way [that's the what] by releasing unreasonable expectations and coming to a more mindful, compassionate view of themselves and others [that's the how]. I'm passionate about helping people release unrealistic expectations and to be more compassionate with themselves. With that in mind, I found it easier to define my business, and, more importantly, my vision for it. As you'll see, my mission statement is flexible enough to accommodate whatever direction I choose to take my business in the future.

Flexibility is the key in coming up with your business plan. Your practice will not be perfect (see what I did there?) and neither will your plan. It's a sketch, not a fully realized photograph or painting of what will happen. And if you do manage to generate a business plan that looks exactly like the end result, you could probably make more money in business consulting and fortune-telling than in private practice.

Another reason to prepare a business plan is that even if you're not seeking loans or other types of investment, you will be asked for the information from other partners. For example, my malpractice insurance has me send in a letter each year regarding the nature of my business and the services it provides. Also, your plan can help you define your "elevator pitch" to use when you're networking.

Here are the elements contained in a business plan:

1. The nature of the business, why it's needed, and why *you're* passionate about it.
2. What you hope to accomplish in your business. What are your goals?
3. What, specifically, are you offering?
4. Who your clients or customers will be.
5. Where you'll find your clients and marketing strategies.
6. Who your competition is and how you're different.
7. Financial needs.

Financial Considerations

Although it's still early in the book, it's a good idea to start thinking about budget and profit, or what will be left over once you've met your financial obligations. You can go ahead and think about what you'd like to pay yourself and include that in the budget, or you can see what obligations you'll have and then add pay on top of it. One thing to remember is that no matter how great or specialized your niche, it will likely take you at least two years to build to a full caseload if you're working full-time, so you'll need to take that into account when you're planning out what you can spend. Just like a home budget, there are some items that are non-negotiable and others that are luxuries (e.g., coffee, water service) that you can add in later. Here is a general outline of expenses, which I'll discuss in more detail in Chapter 6:

Overheads:
Rent
Parking (if not included in rent)
Utilities (if not included in rent)
Housekeeping (if not included in rent)
Telephone
Internet
Office supplies
Environmental comforts like music, water, and coffee service
Payroll if you have employees
Electronic Health Records costs
Credit Card fees
Equipment
Postage

Consultation:
Accountant
Compliance
Legal

Continuing Education:
Professional Memberships
Conferences
Workshops
Travel

Insurance: amounts often determined by landlord and included in the lease:
Malpractice
General liability
Workman's Comp

Licenses:
Business License
State License
Annual Corporation Renewal Fee
Marketing: mostly TBD, but go ahead and start thinking about website design and hosting
Taxes: Note—property taxes refer to the stuff in your office if you're renting
Payroll—yes, even if you're just paying yourself
State Property
County Property
City Property

Some of these are monthly, some annual, and some occasional like continuing education. I've come up with a spreadsheet to help you figure out your budget should you need a little extra help organizing it all. You can download it at www.sleepyintheatl.com/budgettemplate, but read Chapter 6 first.

Conclusion

Tempted to skip the business plan? I don't blame you—it can seem intimidating. And I don't know about you, but when I decide to do something, I can be a "let me get started, and I'll figure it out as I go" type of person. That's how

I write my novels, but as you can imagine, when you're starting a business, that's not the best attitude. There is a saying, "If you fail to plan, then you plan to fail." When I looked it up so I could properly attribute it, I found versions attributed to Benjamin Franklin and Winston Churchill, so it seems like pretty good advice. With regard to your business, taking the time to plan now at the front end will save you a lot of headaches and perhaps even heartaches. I strongly encourage you to fill out what you can on the business plan worksheet and come back to it as ideas occur to you throughout the book. By the end, you may have a mostly complete plan with areas you want to investigate more on your own.

Bibliography

Author's note: there are business plan templates a-plenty online, but I didn't really understand what drove it until I took an online course through Udemy, which has a lot of good courses and frequent sales. I've referenced the course below as well as the Small Business Administration website where you can find more information for free.

Advance Learning. (n.d.). Complete guide to drafting a business plan [Online course]. Retrieved from www.udemy.com/writeabusinessplan/.

U.S. Small Business Administration. (n.d.). Write your business plan. Retrieved from www.sba.gov/starting-business/write-your-business-plan.

Worksheet—Business Plan

Sometimes it's easier to generate a business plan with some more specific questions. Here are the elements and questions to help you clarify them:

1. The nature of the business, why it's needed, and why you're passionate about it. The nature of the business—yes, this is a private practice, but what kind? Will it be a single provider or multiple providers? Housed in a bigger organization or completely independent, as we discussed earlier in this chapter? Write a few sentences to brainstorm what your ideal practice looks like:

Why does the world, or more specifically, your community, need this type of business?

Why do you want to open your practice? What excites you about it? This is important not only for the business plan but also for those days when it seems that frustration awaits you at every turn. Think both about the private practice itself and the work you want to do. For example, if you treat anxiety disorders, what do you love most about working with that population?

2. What you hope to accomplish in your business. What are your goals? Do you envision a part-time or full-time practice? How many patients/clients do you want to see per week? What, roughly, is the salary you'd like to pay yourself? How do you envision this practice changing your community?

3. What, specifically, are you offering? What disorders are you going to focus on treating? As you'll see in future chapters, it's easier to have a specialty than to be a general practitioner. Will you offer individual or group sessions?

Do you treat a specific age group—adult, adolescent, child, geriatric? What modality? Are you a cognitive-behavioral therapist? Dialectical behavioral? Psychodynamic? Sorry, you can't get away with integrative unless you say exactly what you're integrating and how. Whatever therapeutic perspective you choose, how is it the most appropriate for the problem you're going to treat?

4. Who your clients or customers will be. Who do you envision is going to be seeking your services? Think beyond gender, age, and socioeconomic status to what their interests are. For example, in my practice, I seek patients who have a similar philosophy to mine that sleep medications are not meant for long-term use. What kinds of books do your ideal clients read, or what websites do they visit? What are their financial priorities?

5. Where you'll find your clients and marketing strategies. We'll talk about marketing more specifically later in the book, so you don't necessarily need to focus on them here, but go ahead and brainstorm a few. Do you envision getting clients through referrals from other providers? Websites such as Psychology Today, Google searches? If you were to search for a therapist or other provider, what would you do? Can you see yourself doing health fairs or talking to groups at conferences even after talking to people for a living all week?

6. Who your competition is and how you're different. If you're in a part of town like I am where you can't throw a rock without hitting a therapist (it's not recommended to throw rocks at people or just randomly, btw), how are you going to stand out? What services do you offer that are either unique, in high demand, or both? Or do you serve a large population for whom there are insufficient providers? Think about what's special about you, your experience, and what would be hard for other therapists to copy about your style and treatment methods. How are you going to survive as the economy, insurance situations, and technology changes?

7. Financial needs. Think about what financial needs the business will have. This includes insurance (malpractice, general liability, workman's comp), overhead (rent, utilities, etc.; see Chapter 3), materials, and personnel cost. We'll continue to add to this list throughout the book, but go ahead and brainstorm out what you think you'll need here.

Making Your Practice Legit

2

Incorporation

So now that you've decided to start a business, it's time to figure out what legal structure you're going to have. There are people smarter than I am who have looked into all of this, so I highly recommend you check out the U.S. Small Business Administration website to determine which would be best for you (see site link in Bibliography). When you're looking to incorporate, I encourage you to consider two things in particular.

First, remember we are in a litigious society, and sometimes people are all too ready to lawyer up and sue. That's why you want to incorporate—making your company a legal entity of its own helps you to protect your personal assets. One of the most popular types of incorporation structure is the limited liability company, or LLC. It's one of the simplest structures but has some limitations, which brings me to the second point: self-employment taxes. These along with regular income tax can add up to 50 percent of your total income. Ouch!

When you incorporate as an LLC, you're subject to self-employment tax as well as income tax. My accountant advised me instead to set up my business as an S Corporation, or S Corp. There is also a Personal Corporation type of incorporation. Confused yet? As I'll discuss in a future chapter, this is why it's helpful to have an accountant or lawyer help you set everything up. In practical terms, it means my company is taxed as a corporation, but all taxes go through my personal tax returns. Yes, it sounds complicated, but rather than paying myself out of an LLC and being subject to self-employment tax on the entirety of the money made by the practice, I pay myself a salary, which has the usual Medicare and Social Security taxes taken out. I also give myself profit distributions, which are taxed at a lower rate and in some states, may not be at all. This ends up saving money in taxes. Having an S Corp also allows me to write off a certain amount as business expenses and gives me the freedom to add partners to the practice and then pass the practice on to them in the future if I so desire. If you have an LLC, when you leave it or (eek!) die, the company dissolves. On the flip side, I have to indicate I have shareholder meetings and record minutes for them, so there's extra paperwork involved.

As I'm sure I'm going to say an annoying number of times, the rules for all states are different, so it's best to consult an accountant or attorney who's knowledgeable in such matters to figure out what would be the best situation for your practice. Also, it's good to remember that while incorporating protects your personal assets to a certain degree, you will run across situations where they may be at risk. For example, many leases have clauses that hold you and your company responsible for paying off the balance of the lease, should you terminate early. For more information on this, see Box 2.1.

All the Little Numbers

As you've probably figured out from having to deal with taxes and other areas of life, the government runs on numbers. Here are some of the numbers and other legal requirements for you and your practice, especially if you're going to file insurance claims:

Tax I.D. Number or Employer Identification Number (EIN)

This is the number the Internal Revenue Service uses to identify your company for tax purposes. Think of it as your practice's social security number—your TIN is the identification number of your business as an entity. This is also how insurance companies may identify you and one of the easiest ways potential clients can see if you're in a network. You can apply online for your EIN here: http://www.irs.gov/Businesses/Small-Businesses-&-Self-Employed/Apply-for-an-Employer-Identification-Number-%28EIN%29-Online.

The National Provider Identifier (NPI)

This is a separate number in a different database. You will likely end up having a different NPI number as an individual and as a practice, especially if you're going to grow your practice to include other providers. Insurance claims often require both the TIN and NPI numbers. How do you get one? Go here: https://nppes.cms.hhs.gov/NPPES/Welcome.do.

Business License

No matter where you are, if you're a business, you're going to need a license. Just like your professional license, you'll pay a fee to a local structure annually for permission to do business in that area. The fun part? Business license fees and the process to acquire a business license will vary from area to area, and sometimes it's not always clear where you have to go for them. For example, when I started my practice, I was in a city that had recently formed and was trying to attract business, so its fees were relatively low, about $180. The process for getting the business license was easy—bring the forms required by the website, got to city hall, give them money, and *voilà*. Then I moved my practice closer to home into an already established city that is notorious for high taxes. My business license fees more than doubled to $425. So did the length of time to get a business license. Between getting various pieces of paper signed by various government officials and having a fire warden inspection, it took about a week. Then whenever I renewed my license, which has to be done annually, I ended up sending everything in, waiting, and eventually having to call that department and then go to City Hall to get the license.

My most recent experience was the most expensive and time consuming. I moved my office all of 1.2 miles, but this change took me out of the city and into an unincorporated area, which meant I needed to acquire a county business license. Silly me, I thought that the process couldn't get any more ridiculous. Nope. To get a county business license, I had to first gather a bunch of paperwork, get it notarized, and then go to the county offices to apply for a building permit even though I was moving into the space without any sort of construction or build-out. The permit fee was $475. They then sent me across the room to the business license department, where I turned in yet more paperwork, but I couldn't get the license yet because I needed a certificate of occupancy (COI). In order to obtain that, I had to then wait two weeks for the building permit to be approved—remember, there was nothing to actually approve—then call to schedule a fire marshal inspection. They schedule you for the "next available" time slot, which is within one business day, but they don't tell you what time the fire marshal will show up. After I passed the inspection, I got to return to the county offices, turn in the signed card, and get the certificate of occupancy. I made another trip to the county offices, took the COI to the business license window and traded it and about $160 for my business license. Which I got to renew less than a month later in January. At least the renewal process was by mail.

Moral of the story—when you get down to local government bureaucracy, it can be a very frustrating experience. Be sure to give yourself plenty of time to complete this step. I would recommend starting at least a month before you plan on opening your doors and actually conducting business.

Professional License

This will be required before you get your business license. I'm assuming if you're reading this book, you're licensed as a professional in the state you want to practice in. If not, this would be your first step. In some states, certain types of Master's-level providers can't practice independently, so check your state laws.

Business Registration

This is a form you need to fill out with your state's Secretary of State office along with a fee (of course) to register your business as a legal entity. You also need to renew it annually. You can register any business name as long as there isn't another business with the exact same name in your state.

Just when you've gotten your numbers figured out, it's time to ponder forms. These are the ones you need to be most familiar with:

W-9

Whenever you do work for an entity, whether it's seeing patients for an insurance company, doing consulting for a corporation, writing a book, or otherwise provide services, they'll likely require you to do a W-9. Like many government forms, this one has about half a page of stuff for you to fill out and two pages of instructions. Its purpose is for you to tell them in a legal way that you have a Tax I.D. number, you're a U.S. citizen, and you are not subject to backup tax withholding. How would you know if you're subject to backup tax withholding? The IRS will tell you.

W-2

If you've worked for someone as a salaried or hourly employee, you've received a W-2. This is the form you need for your taxes to show how much you've earned and plug in what's been withheld. If you have salaried or hourly employees, you are required to give them this form at the beginning of the year. This is one reason I recommend you use a payroll company. We'll talk more about this in the next chapter.

1099

If you've worked as a contractor, you probably got this at the beginning of the year, and like the W-2, you need to give it to your contractors at that time.

I-9

This is a form you need to have on file for all your employees to show you've checked their citizenship status and have verified it with the required number of forms of I.D.

Oh, and one VERY IMPORTANT thing to remember about corporate taxes, once you get to that point, is that they must be filed by March 15 every year to avoid a late penalty. Also, they must be filed before your personal tax returns.

Finally, there's insurance. I'm going to stick with talking about insurance for your business. If you're jumping into this full-time and don't have a spouse or partner whose health insurance you can go on, you'll have to find your own health, dental, life, etc. insurance. The business insurance was a bit of a shock to me, not only the amount of insurance I had to have but also the prices. When you sign a commercial lease, there's often a clause that you have to carry liability and workman's compensation insurance to a certain amount. It's not cheap. So, here's what you need:

Malpractice Insurance

This is necessary whether you work for yourself or not. Some employers will get a policy for you, but when you have your own practice, you need your own policy.

General Liability Insurance

This covers you should someone injure themselves at your practice, if your business is interrupted for whatever reason, and is general all-around protection.

Workman's Compensation Insurance

This is necessary in case an employee hurts themselves while working for you. In my experience, this has typically been issued along with the general liability insurance but costs extra. If you don't have any employees, you can skip this one and negotiate with your landlord to drop this requirement.

If you're doing exposures or otherwise using your automobile for therapy, you may need a different type of car insurance. Your auto insurance agent should be able to tell you about that.

What's in a Name?

One major decision that many people don't think about until they get to a decision point is what to name your practice. On the surface, this seems like an easy thing. Many practitioners simply go for the simplest option—their name. For example, you may decide to call your company John Smith, LLC. There are a few things to consider. Yes, this is where I confess another mistake I've made.

First, is your practice name going to help you stand out? The mental health field, in spite of its many frustrations, is a crowded one, so when people are perusing lists of practices, it's best to give them an idea of what you do. For example, my practice is named Atlanta Insomnia and Behavioral Health Services, P.C. Detailed, yes. When someone calls, they know exactly what I do and what my practice focuses on. If you do decide to go with a descriptive name, do an online search and make sure it's available.

Second, does your practice name allow you to have some flexibility? If you're absolutely sure you're going to stay a solo practitioner for the rest of your practice's life, and that's the only type of business activity you'll conduct under that entity, using your name is fine. However, I've known a few people who have had to change their company names from something like John Smith, LLC to Smith and Associates, LLC when they got so busy they needed help handling all their referrals. Changing a business name requires paperwork and can be a hassle, not to mention changing signage, letterhead, and marketing materials to reflect it. This would be another reason to go for a descriptive name rather than just your name—bringing on more people won't change it.

Third, make sure that whatever you choose, your business name doesn't exceed 30 characters. Why? Because a lot of government forms including tax forms limit the number of characters. As you can see from my practice name, it's a bit long. My accountant had to come up with a squished version to use as a legal name that I have to look up every time I have to use it, like on a W-9 when someone requests one. Most recently, I found that my company name won't fit in its entirety on the hallway sign in my new office, and the sign out front is hard to read. The long business name strikes again.

You'll see a term "DBA" or "doing business as." This is a name that's different from your own name or legal entity name. So, for example, on my W-9, I put the squished name of my business on the "Legal Name" line and "Atlanta Insomnia & Behavioral Health Services, P.C." on the "Doing Business As" line. See the U.S. Small Business Association website reference for more details.

I'm going to talk more about marketing in a subsequent chapter, but I do want to encourage you at this point to return to the mission statement you started pondering in Chapter 1. Do you have an opportunity for your practice name to reflect that? It's also a good idea to revisit the mission statement as you go through the process of setting up your practice and then in the early days to remind yourself why you're doing this. As I described in the introduction, having your own practice is not always easy, and there will be days when you question your own sanity for going into this profession. Reviewing your mission statement is one way to encourage yourself, but it also helps to have the reminder in your practice name, which you will see daily.

Accounts and Whatnot

I'll talk more about financial matters in Chapter 6, but since setting up accounts falls under initial setup, I wanted to mention them here. Once you've gotten your Articles of Incorporation from your Secretary of State's office, it's time to set up your business accounts. It's good to do this as soon as possible because, as we'll discuss in a later chapter, it will be easier to keep an accurate record of what you've spent. I have two bank accounts, a business checking account and a business savings account. I use the checking account for operational expenses, and the savings account is there in case I need extra money one month. It's also good for storing money for big purchases, conferences, and other large expenses that only come along occasionally. I recommend having these in the same bank so you can use the website interface to transfer money between the two of them.

While some business owners may prefer to only use checks or cash, it's a good idea to also have a business credit card. Cash can be hard to keep track of, although you probably do want to keep some on hand, and it can be easy to forget to get receipts for cash purchases. I end up ordering a lot of my supplies online—including testing forms—which is very difficult, if not impossible, to do without a credit card. Many cards also offer some sort of fraud and/or purchase protection, which gives you an extra layer of safety when dealing with a new merchant you may not be familiar with. While you can't use credit card statements the same way you use receipts for purchases, they can be useful to help you track your money, and the monthly reconciliation process can be helpful in keeping you on track with your budget.

Another advantage of having a business credit card is that it will help you establish your business credit score. Just like individuals, businesses have credit. I found this out the hard way when the bank that issued my first business card closed, leaving me without a business card for an upcoming conference trip. I immediately applied for another one but got turned down by the first company I approached because I'd only been in business for less than two years, and I hadn't established enough credit. I did get a card from a different company, and I still have it. I pay it off every month and use the rewards points, either to treat myself or for statement credit.

Conclusion

Are you intimidated yet? Don't worry if you are. One way to keep the anxiety down is to start getting organized if you haven't already done so, even if you don't have your office space yet. What do you need to do?

First, start tracking expenses and figuring out how you're going to organize them now. I kept a banker's box with my startup receipts in folders labeled "Furniture," "Computer/Printer," "Incorporation," "Licenses," etc. Second, set up a spreadsheet for furniture, equipment, and other stuff that you're buying now and back it up online through something like Google Docs or Dropbox, so if your office contents are destroyed in a flood or fire, you have an inventory to show your insurance company. You can also help keep insurance costs low because if you don't give your agent an exact number for what it will cost to replace your stuff, they'll assign an arbitrary amount that will likely be way too high, which will drive up the premium.

Whatever you do, keep the worksheet handy and either put the login sites and passwords for the various items on the worksheet or set up something like LastPass to keep track of them. No, you can't use the same password for everything, as you'll see in a later chapter. Make them different and as complex as the sites will allow. The ideal is lowercase letters, uppercase letters, numbers, symbols, and Druidic incantations. Okay, I'm kidding about the incantations, but an ideal password will contain the others. You'll only need to log in to some of the sites like the Secretary of State's office once a year, and if you can remember passwords for that long, great. I can't.

Now that we've talked about the tedious government stuff, let's move on to something fun—setting up your physical office space.

Box 2.1 Interview with the Expert: Linda Collett

Linda Collett is a business attorney in Atlanta, and she was kind enough to put together this section for me. While it's not an interview per se, it's definitely pertinent and useful information. Linda is also the person who taught me the phrase, "You don't know what you don't know" (L. Collett, personal communication, October 26, 2016).

Protecting your personal assets from the debts and liabilities of your business is a two-step process. First, you have to create a liability shield and then you have to maintain that liability shield. Having a liability shield means that you don't have to spend your personal money or liquidate your personal assets such as your home, car, or family heirlooms in order to pay the debts or liabilities that your company can't pay.

You create a liability shield by forming a business entity such as a limited liability company or corporation. If you collect money for the services you provide, you are sole proprietorship and do not have a liability shield. Similarly, if you and another person decide to go into business together without forming an LLC or corporation, you do not have a liability shield. And what's worse, each partner can obligate the partnership and you have unlimited personal liability for the debts and liabilities incurred by your partner.

Once you have a liability shield, you need to maintain it so that you don't unintentionally expose your personal assets to the risks of your business. Here's what you need to do to maintain your entity so that your liability shield remains intact.

1. Renew your entity's registration with the Secretary of State every year.

2. Make sure your company is capitalized adequately, which means that it has enough money for its expenses and it has sufficient insurance to cover any claims that someone may make against it. At the very least you'll want a general liability policy to cover your office and professional liability insurance to cover your professional services.

3. Follow company or corporate formalities. This means that you are operating your company with formal books, records, and decision-making processes and you aren't operating your company as an "alter ego" for yourself as an individual. If you form a corporation rather than an LLC, there are lots of statutes that dictate the formalities you need to follow. For example, the law in most jurisdictions requires that the shareholders and directors of a corporation have annual meetings, even if there is only one shareholder and one director in the corporation.

4. Keep your personal and company money separate. This means having separate business and personal bank accounts and not paying any personal expenses from your business account.

5. Sign contracts as an agent of your LLC or corporation rather than as an individual. This means first of all making sure that in your company formation documents you have the authority to sign contracts on behalf of your company. Then, you want to make sure that your company (not you) is named as the party to any agreement and when you sign the agreement you want to sign your name and use your officer title, assuming that officer position has been created in your formation documents and you have been elected or appointed to that position. If you have an LLC, you usually will be safe signing as a "Member" unless your Operating Agreement says that Members can't bind the company. If you own a corporation, you want to make sure that you are named as a director of the corporation and appointed as an officer, then you can sign your name as a "Director" or as the officer.

6. Limit personal guaranties. A personal guaranty is where you agree to pay an obligation if your company can't pay it. Personal guaranties will show up most commonly in leases, trade credit applications, company credit cards, and bank loans. Sometimes you can negotiate to eliminate the personal guaranty but not always. In that case,

just know that you are intentionally breaching your liability shield and agreeing to put your own money at risk if for any reason your company can't pay the obligation.

Areas where private medical or psychological practices could use a business attorney, which are also areas where they are particularly at risk, include:

1. Formation of your LLC or corporate entity. As discussed above, it's really important to make sure your entity is formed correctly so you have a liability shield and your personal assets are protected. It is particularly important to have an attorney help you if you are forming a corporation because there's a lot more to it than simply register- ing it with the Secretary of State and if you don't have all the proper documents and an organizational meeting, you don't have a properly formed corporation with the liability shield you're expecting.

2. Co-owner agreements. If you're going to go into practice with one or more other people you will definitely want to hire an attorney to help you talk through how you are going to run the company together. It's always better (and less expensive in the long run) to discuss and negotiate everything on the front end while everyone is on good terms and getting along rather than after a problem has arisen and the relationship is strained. A few of the many issues that should be decided include the following: the services each person will perform; how much money each person will contribute; how and when money will be distributed from the company; how you will manage the company; whether an owner can sell his or her interest in the company to anyone including a competitor; what happens to a person's ownership interest if they die, are disabled, resign, or retire. An attorney can offer suggestions and then document your agreements in an Operating Agreement, Buy-Sell Agreement, Shareholders' Agreement or some other document appropriate for your business.

3. Lease review and negotiation. If you don't own your own office building or condo, you will likely need to lease office space. A lease agreement provided by the landlord will usually be very favorable to the landlord and often in ways that tenants don't even realize until it's too late and a problem has arisen. This is a document that

you should always have reviewed by an attorney before signing. But don't just have the attorney review it for you, pay the attorney for an extra hour or so to explain to you what you're actually agreeing to in the lease as well as any provisions that the attorney would recommend that you try to negotiate with the landlord.

Bibliography

National Plan and Provider Enumeration System. (n.d.). National provider identifier. Retrieved from https://nppes.cms.hhs.gov/NPPES/Welcome.do.

U.S. Small Business Administration. (n.d.). Choose your business structure. Retrieved from https://www.sba.gov/starting-business/choose-your-business-structure.

U.S. Small Business Administration. (n.d.). Register your business name. Retrieved from https://www.sba.gov/starting-business/choose-register-your-business/register-your-business-name.

Worksheet—Before You Start, You Need:

Are you overwhelmed with details yet? This worksheet is a checklist of the things you'll need to have in place for your business before you start. Go ahead and write down the numbers so you have them all in one place. Trust me, you'll need them later, especially if you're going to file insurance.

___ Business Name:
___ Tax I.D.:
___ National Provider Identifier (NPI)
   ___ Individual:
   ___ Group:

Licenses:
___ Professional License
___ Business License
___ Business Registration (find your Articles of Incorporation if you're a P.C. or Letter of Formation if you're an LLC, print them out, and keep them in a safe place)

Accounts:
___ Business Checking
___ Business Savings
___ Business Credit Card

Insurance:
___ Malpractice Insurance
___ General Liability Insurance
___ Workman's Comp Insurance (if applicable)

An Office of One's Own

3

One of the joys of having one's own practice is getting to set up your own space to be just the way you want it. I got a lesson in just how sensitive I am to aesthetics when I was in graduate school. The therapy rooms in our psychology clinic were tiny cinder block boxes with two chairs and a little table in them. The cinder block was painted, but I was sure the rats in the biopsych lab on the sixth floor had cheerier accommodations. I will admit that I didn't do my best therapy as a student—and who does?—but not only because I was just starting out. It's very difficult to encourage someone when you're both staring at painted cinderblock. I suspect there may have been some negative associations with the decor. My high school walls were also of painted cinderblock, so perhaps I had some lingering anxiety reactions. Consequently, when I started my own practice, my only space requirement was that the walls would be plastered or have drywall on them.

Since then, I've come to expand my requirements for what my practice space has, although smooth walls are still a must. Thankfully, they're easy to find outside of trendy bare-walled loft-style spaces, which have other characteristics that are not ideal for therapy practices.

That brings me to my first topic—types of office space.

Types of Office Space

When I was originally writing this chapter, I was looking at different office spaces with another allied health professional with an eye on developing a multi-disciplinary health-focused practice. Is that vague enough? He's a dietitian, and we each have our own ideas of what sort of arrangement we'd like. I'm coming from a two-office suite in a Class B building, and he's coming from a shared office space run by a corporation that allows him to rent space in different locations for a monthly fee. During this process, we've both had to really consider not only what our needs are currently, but also how we want our practice(s) to grow.

When you look for office spaces, here are some terms you're likely to come across and what they mean:

Class A/B building: According to the website of the Building Owners and Management Association (BOMA), this is the definition of a Class A Building: "Most prestigious buildings competing for premier office users with rents above average for the area. Buildings have high quality standard finishes, state of the art systems, exceptional accessibility and a definite market presence."

As you can imagine, Class B and Class C buildings step down from there with regard to rent costs but also amenities, systems, and finishes. I liked Weslee Knapp's explanation of the differences in Box 3.1.

I've seen the difference between the building classes in my own office rental history. When I started my practice, it was in a Class A building, which was lovely, sophisticated, and warm with marble accents in the lobby. It was no problem for my wheelchair-bound patients to get in and out of the building or use the facilities. When I moved to a different part of town, I ended up in a Class B building, which was definitely older, having been built in the 1970s, and less accessible. For example, the only wheelchair-accessible bathroom was in the basement, and I had to have one of the doors in my office widened to meet width requirements. The building has since gone through elevator, lobby, and climate control upgrades, so I think it's trying to compete with the Class A buildings in the area. The biggest change was in the lobby, which went from basic wood and linoleum to all white and gray marble with modern metal accents. Going into it was like walking into a giant ice cube. The building may have been reclassified by now.

When you're looking for space, think about how many offices you need. Will it just be you? Do you want room for storage or to grow? Other considerations may include whether you need a larger space in which to run groups.

In the Atlanta area, we have several types of office spaces available. One type is the traditional office space like my previous situations. There are some advantages to this kind of space including:

- No hidden costs for utilities, etc. Everything is included in the rent.
- On-call maintenance. Aside from the singing air vent, things were fixed fairly quickly.

- Moderate safety. I had a neighbor on one side, who I don't think I could've counted on, and the office on the other side was vacant, but at least I knew I wasn't alone on the floor. Plus, there was a security guard for the building after hours.
- Storage space in the basement. Again, this isn't an option in every large office building, but it was nice to have somewhere to store those files we're supposed to keep for seven years.
- Configuration and decorating options at the front end of the lease. Be aware that if you're going to be engaging in major "buildout" like moving walls, the cost of the construction will likely end up increasing your rent.

Some of the disadvantages of the traditional office space can include:

- Noisy neighbors. The neighbor on one side of me was a lawyer who liked to have, shall we say, animated conversations with less than professional language. When she or her employees were in her conference room, the sound carried through the air vents to my office. I mentioned this to her one day, and let's just say she was not receptive to the feedback.
- Little power to make changes after the initial office setup.
- Rent goes up yearly.
- In some spaces, no control of temperature or climate.

Many of the mental health specialists in my area share space in small houses that they own as a group or rent. Some advantages of house arrangements could include:

- Ample free parking.
- No neighbors within close distance, above, or below you.
- Cozy feel.
- Kitchen space with plumbing, which makes for a nice break room.
- Control of climate.

Some disadvantages may be:

- Limited parking.
- Responsibility for utilities.
- If owned, responsibility for mortgage, insurance, etc. You also may need to ensure it's zoned properly for your business.
- Need to manage cleaning service and trash/recycling removal.
- Yard service may not be included. If you're in a colder climate, it also includes snow removal.

- Less responsive maintenance, especially if you're renting and the owner is offsite.
- Might be harder to find/give directions.
- Load-bearing walls may limit possible internal configurations.

Smaller office buildings offer a combination of the advantages and disadvantages described above. I've just moved into a three-story office building that's owned and managed by a small company. The landlord has been mostly responsive as we've been settling in and found problems, and he's managing the signage. The bathroom and other common areas are cleaned, but our office suite isn't, and we had to hire our own housekeeper, who comes once a week. If we want our trash emptied more frequently, we have to do it ourselves. I do appreciate that the building is easy to find, and parking is free and plentiful. I also have a bigger space, and there is a room with a sink that we're using for a post-doc office/break room. Alas, there isn't a "bat door," as my colleague calls it, for us to be able to sneak out to the bathroom without having to go through the waiting room.

In small towns or rural areas, the options for practice space are more limited. One of the major factors to consider is whether clients can go in and out of your office without losing confidentiality.

Some mental health professionals practice out of their homes. The main reasons I've avoided this sort of arrangement are that I don't have room, my husband works from home, and I also have two cats. As you may know, even if you shut animals away in another part of the building, people with particularly sensitive allergies may still be affected. It's also more difficult for people to go in and out of private residences discreetly, although I know therapists who use a back parking area and door or other solutions. For example, I once saw a therapist who had a huge hedge in front of her house for patients to park behind. Plus, there are boundary and privacy issues to consider. If you don't see a population that prompts concern about patient stalking or spying, then by all means consider a house space. Just be aware that if you decide to write off that space for taxes, you will be penalized if it looks like that space is ever used for anything else if you are audited. Business expert Rebecca Beaton once relayed a story about someone being fined for writing off a desk space in their house because it had a dog bed, which indicated it was personal, not business space, under it.

Layout and Safety

Let's assume you've acquired your space and have access to it. What do you need and how do you set it up?

When I moved into my first solo office space in 2010, I had to buy everything myself. That meant I needed to figure out how to furnish a two-office space on a budget. The first thing I did was make a list of what I would need.

The second step was to scour the used office furniture stores in town to find the basics such as filing cabinets. My thought was that since they wouldn't be visible to patients, it didn't matter if they were a little dinged up, and that was exactly the case for the filing cabinet I had in my basement storage space for closed patient files. One particularly nice find was a used Herman Miller Aeron chair, which I bought for much less than the new price. It was a little bit of a splurge, but I decided it was worth it due to my back problems. The therapist chairs in my office are also nicer because those are where the provider will sit most of the time.

Furniture can be the most expensive purchase. For example, nice waiting room chairs can often run into several hundred dollars each. Yes, each. I splurged with two of mine, but for the other two, I went to consignment furniture stores to find some nice basic leather chairs. Ditto for lamps, which can also be ridiculously expensive. For other furnishings, I went to a factory-direct store, where I got a discount for buying several items at once. I'm not a decorator, but my best friend is, and we talked about the atmosphere I was trying to create and the colors I would like to use. I went with a pretty neutral palette with jewel tone accents. I also decided I would like a balance of straight lines and curves and found furniture that fit that aesthetic.

It's also important to consider client comfort, both physical and psychological. When I bought the furniture for my office, I chose it according to what felt good for me. I'm fairly tall for a woman, and it soon became apparent that my couch was too deep for some of my shorter clients. Consequently, I have lots of pillows for people to stack behind them if needed. It's also good to have an option for people who may have back problems. I've sometimes switched chairs with clients so they could sit in mine, which has a back support. As with everything, be flexible. I had one client whose back sometimes allowed her to be comfortable only when sitting on the floor, so that's what we did.

As for other kinds of comfort, I attempted to create a calming atmosphere. I chose colors that were neutral and/or soothing, and I never use the fluorescent lights. I also keep white noise going in my office, and my office manager plays soft jazz or classical music in the waiting room.

Did it work? A few months after I leased my office space, someone on the floor mentioned they called it "the sleepy office" because when they got peeks in there, they noticed the soft green color of the walls and the white noise. Since I'm a behavioral sleep medicine specialist, I think I succeeded in achieving my desired aesthetic.

At the very least, you need somewhere for you to sit while doing therapy, somewhere for the patient/client to sit, and a surface on which to put materials, coffee, etc. I've just recreated my graduate school therapy rooms in my head—shudder. I also have a desk, an end table for me, an end table on which there are tissues and a coaster for the patients to use, an office chair, a bookcase, and a side table/printer/telephone stand by the desk. All of these are items that help me to feel comfortable in my space and also produce the feel of a living room/office rather than a treatment room.

As for office setup, this is where comfort needs to be balanced with risk management and client confidentiality. The therapist should always sit closest to the door in case a quick escape is needed, and there should be nothing between your seat and the door. Thankfully, I haven't had to face the situation of needing to escape and hope I never will. If you're scheduling people electronically, you will also need to have the computer screen facing away from the patient so they can't see other patients' names on the calendar. A privacy screen—a piece of plastic you can fit over the screen that only allows the screen to be seen head-on—can be helpful in this case. If you have patient materials on your desk—for example, if you're working on an assessment report—you should keep those materials in a folder or otherwise out of sight when other patients are in your office. Finally, remember that many office spaces have after-hours cleaning crews, so it's best to put up patient materials at the end of the day. When I was in a larger office building, I had to ask the management to please tell the cleaning crew not to come into my office until after 7:00 p.m.

Part of getting a business license in many places will be a visit from a fire marshal. When you set up your office, make sure that the path to the exit is clear and that there's no way for anyone to get locked in and be unable to reach the exit. Some places may also require you to have a lighted sign over the exit door.

Office Space Wish List

Now that I've been in an office space, here are the things I've greatly appreciated or have wished for:

Designated Storage Space

My last office had a walk-in closet behind the administrator's desk with a lockable door. It contained the copy/fax machine, mini fridge, microwave, and filing cabinet as well as miscellaneous items, such as shelves with hooks for lunch totes or jackets and space for flatware, tea and coffee boxes, and mugs. It's one area we didn't have to worry about keeping neat, but we did anyway. I also had a secure storage space in the basement of the building for closed patient files, spare pillows for my couch, and other items not frequently needed in the office. I've now gone to HIPAA-compliant secure online backup, so I don't need that extra storage space. However, my current office doesn't have a closet, so we had to make sure the file cabinet locks were in good working order when we moved, and I had to get a little cabinet for tea and such. At least one office in the suite had cabinets for other things, so we had a place for cups, spoons, etc.

Back Entrance

In my first office arrangement, the providers entered the office suite through a back door in their copy/file room. That way patients wouldn't see if we were running late or if we had to duck out to use the restroom. For those of us who are strong introverts, it can be helpful to have control over when you interact with your patients and not have to do so by walking through the waiting room on your way out to run an errand. I didn't even think about this when I rented my second office space and came to regret it.

Climate Control in the Office

When I was in a large office building, I had no control over the temperature in my office since one section of the HVAC system serviced several different offices. Changes were made via some sort of central mechanism. Some days my office was freezing. Other days it was horribly stuffy. Since I was on the tenth floor and the windows wouldn't open, I had no control over temperature aside from opening and closing window blinds and blocking air vents with pillows.

Good Soundproofing between Offices and Suites

While there is some soundproofing in the form of ceiling insulation, there is still noise bleed-through. This is a challenge no matter what type of space you have. Go ahead and invest in some good white noise machines.

Mail Delivery Straight to and Pickup Directly from the Office

In my first office arrangement, someone had to go to the mail room in the basement to pick up the mail. Since this was before any of us had direct deposit from insurance companies, the daily mail run was very important. In my last situation, the mail came directly to the office, which I much prefer, until just a few months before I moved. Apparently the office building was the last holdout, and the post office made them comply. So, this wish may not be doable at this point. Still, it was nice while it lasted. At least in my current office the mailboxes are on the same floor and not too far away.

Internal Hallway

It's really nice to have extra space between me and the waiting room. This probably gets back to the Type A personality thing, but in my previous office, where my office was right off the waiting room, it would bug me when clients would just stroll into my office or would call out when they got there if my office manager was out. Having a hallway provides a nice boundary and allows me to have control of the timing of the interaction.

Ensuite Bathroom

When I was on internship, one rotation was the most desired among the interns, not because of the supervisor or the topic area, but because the intern office, being a former hospital room, had both a window and a bathroom. The rest of the rotation was great, too—it's where I had my first exposure to Acceptance and Commitment Therapy—but having my own bathroom? Pretty sweet.

Break Room

The first office situation I was in had a break room with sink, dishwasher, and a large table. It was nice to be able to get out of my office and eat lunch, and I really liked having the sink to rinse stuff out and get water for my plants.

Receptionist Area That Can Be Closed Off

If your office manager or administrator needs to make telephone calls where they'll be saying a patient's name out loud, it's best for them to be in an area where no one can overhear them. This is typically not an issue, but I have some clients who arrive very early for their appointments.

The Government Requires …

If you take government-sponsored insurance, it's important to ensure your office space is ADA-compliant. Actually, considering that as psychologists, we do try to make our services accessible to the widest range of clients possible, it's good to be aware of and try to follow the guidelines even if you don't accept government insurance plans. What is ADA? The Americans with Disabilities Act was passed in the 1970s in order to remove barriers that people with disabilities face when trying to access services. The ADA website has a great downloadable PDF document with guidelines for small businesses (U.S. Small Business Association Office of Entrepreneurial Management, 1999), so I'm going to give you the summary here. One thing to consider is that states or localities may have stricter guidelines than those listed here.

These are things to ensure your office space includes even before you move in and to ask for if they don't:

Wide enough parking spaces and handicap-accessible parking.

Handicap-accessible entrance. In other words, make it so that people don't have to go up steps to get to your office and that there are ramps on the curb from the parking lot. If your office isn't on the first floor, the building should have an elevator.

Thirty-six-inch-wide doors to accommodate wheelchairs and walkers. I had to have one of the office doors in my last space widened for this reason.

Door handles that can be opened by people with limited hand and arm strength and mobility. I didn't even think about this one until I found this checklist. That explains why all the handles in my current office are latches, not knobs.

Thirty-six-inch-wide lanes for travel within the office.

Check-in and check-out desk that isn't more than 36 inches high.

Adequate space for patients in wheelchairs in the office or chairs that can be moved to make room for them.

Another thing to consider is accessible bathrooms. In my last office space, the only accessible toilets were in the basement. My office was on the tenth floor. On the rare occasion I had someone in a wheelchair come in, it was a pain for them to use the facilities.

Nuts, Bolts, and Utilities

Phone Stuff

I didn't realize until I was talking to my husband about it—and failing to convey exactly what I need—that setting up an office phone arrangement is not necessarily intuitive. At the very least, you need to have some sort of way for patients to get in touch with you confidentially, to leave messages if you're not available, and for you to communicate with other providers. That said, you may be able to get away with just a phone line for a little while longer, but as the world shifts to electronic health records and telemental health, the old days of offices with just phones are passing quickly, and you'll need the internet eventually. Here are some telecommunication options from the least to the most complicated for your practice:

1. A dedicated practice cell phone. The advantage to this solution is that it's simple and straightforward, and if you have a smartphone, you can even use it to manage email. The disadvantages, however, are many. For example, if your phone rings in the middle of the night, is it an emergency, or is it an insomniac calling to make an appointment change? Also, what if your phone gets stolen, breaks, or goes for a swim (you know what I'm talking about)? It can take a while to get a replacement, not to mention the potential for major confidentiality breaches. I know of a couple of practitioners who make use of Google Voice, which allows them a separate number for their regular cell phone—so if something happens to their phone, they can simply send the calls to another number or device. I used Google Voice for a while for my after-hours line, but one thing I didn't like about it was that the incoming calls were random assigned numbers, so I could never set my phone to only allow Google Voice numbers through if I was asleep. Also, Google won't sign a business associate agreement, which we'll get into later, and if you do decide to go with a more traditional phone system or VOIP in the future, porting your number out can be difficult. One of my colleagues just tried to port out his Google Voice number to a VOIP service and couldn't do it because he didn't have bills from them.

2. A land line with office phone system. This is a more traditional option and one I had for a long time. You can get a regular phone and allow the voicemail to be with the carrier, which is the simplest arrangement. However, I have an office manager, so I needed her to be able to answer the phones and transfer calls if necessary. I also wanted a system with

separate boxes for her, me, and another provider. In order to do this, I had to buy a telephone system, which I got used and which lasted for a few years until the handsets started dying. The major disadvantages of this arrangement were that we didn't have a way to handle phone calls as they came in during a major winter storm, so we had to keep calling the voicemail remotely, and the cost of the phone system itself. We also couldn't call from the phone system remotely. Sometimes you need to call clients from outside the office, and while you can set your cell phone to hide your number, occasionally people don't accept calls from hidden or private numbers.

3. A landline with an office phone system and the internet. Because it's a good idea to have the internet. My office is in a place that has strange dead spots for many carriers, and for a while I was with one that required me to stand by my office window to talk on my cell phone. I definitely couldn't handle my electronic health records on my carrier's signal, and the business itself requires a lot of email.

4. Internet and VOIP system. This is my current configuration. VOIP, or Voice Over Internet Protocol, is essentially a way to make telephone calls over the internet. When my old phone system started dying, I looked into other options and found that to pay for just the internet and leasing a VOIP system ended up being about the same cost as my previous internet and telephone service together. I got a nicer phone system I didn't have to buy and that was covered should anything happen to the equipment. My VOIP phone system looks just like a regular office phone system with desk phone sets that resemble the office phones we had previously with bigger screens. My favorite feature on my current system is the silent monitor, which means that when my administrator isn't there, I can see who's calling her phone from my desk and decide whether to grab it or not. It also has the usual stuff like voicemail. One of the really neat things about my VOIP system is that if we were to have a major weather event that keeps us at home, my administrator and I could bring our desk phones home, plug them into our internet, enter our IP addresses (easily found with websites like IP Chicken) into the system, and take calls and manage the schedule from there.

One thing to be aware of is that even in this internet age, offices may not come pre-wired. My second office had apparently belonged to a couple of old-school lawyers who didn't bother with that newfangled internet thing, or maybe they just used wireless. I had to pay for someone to come in and run internet and phone lines through the walls, as well as set up the phone system I had before I went to VOIP. When I moved into my current office, I found that while it had been previously wired—and the real estate agent had verbally assured me and my colleague it was "completely wired"—someone had gone in and cut the wires at the wall jacks, then removed the cabling. So, while I made do with wireless—which my VOIP phones wouldn't work on—I had to scramble to find someone to come out and re-install the wires. One contractor told me that sometimes businesses will cut cables or remove them to spite the landlord or the next tenant, and another contractor said that people will take the wires because they can sell them for the copper inside.

So, here's my advice—establish with the landlord whether the category 5 cabling is already in place for the Ethernet jacks. If so, get the assurance of the place being "completely wired" in writing (which I mistakenly did not) or negotiate with the landlord for them to cover the cost or give you a break on rent to reimburse you for it. When you take possession of your space, unscrew some of the covers and make sure the wiring is there and connected. It's better to find out that way than when you plug in your fancy VOIP phone and nothing happens.

Taking Money

We like to get paid for our services, and I believe we should make it as easy as possible for people. I don't know if there are statistics on this, but my thought is that we are much more likely to collect payment from someone while they're in the office than we are once they leave. What I'm leading up to is that while it would be nice to not lose a percentage to the credit card companies, at this point, it's a necessary evil for doing business. Still, I'm going to give you all the options:

1. Only accepting cash or checks. The advantage to this is, as I've mentioned, you get to keep all your money. The disadvantages are that many people don't have much, if any, cash with them, and a lot of people don't carry their checkbooks anymore. Not taking credit cards is such a rarity at this point that you need to be very clear and up front with them *when they schedule the appointment* that they will need to be prepared to pay with one of these other methods and then say it again during the reminder call/email if you do that. Then remember what we do—emotionally distressed and/or sleep-deprived people are often not as organized or prepared as they would like to be. If a client still shows up without a way to pay, you'll have to make a very awkward decision—do you see them and

trust they'll pay you later, or do you reschedule the appointment, which means you'll risk losing them as a patient? Once you add up that lost potential revenue, you may come to the conclusion that the financial hit to take cards is worth it.

2. Using a device that plugs into your phone and allows you to use some sort of mobile payment system. The beauty of these setups is their simplicity—plug the card reader into your phone or tablet, run your charges, and know that no matter what the charge, you'll be paying a flat percentage. The chip card readers are pretty cool, too. They light up and make noise. Yes, I'm easily entertained.

    The disadvantages—I use Square for my writing, and I think I've lost at least three readers when I took them out of the office to run book sales. Another disadvantage is that they charge a lot more for keyed-in transactions—so if you're running a card you have on file or if someone doesn't have their card with them—and refunds can also mean a big financial hit for the merchants. These systems also don't have very high PCI compliance ratings, which is essentially a method by which data security is measured. Finally, rather than deducting the fees once a month like a more traditional credit card system, some of these systems deduct them daily, so entering everything into the accounting software takes an extra step and balancing the bank statement takes longer, although you will find your mental math improves.

3. I've recently gone back to a more traditional credit card system, and I'm still trying to decide if it's less expensive and more convenient than my mobile reader. The setup fees were kind of high— $100 for the card-sliding device AND another $100 to set up the online portion that goes with my Electronic Health Records (EHR) and the patient portal I keep saying I'm going to set up. The advantages are the ability to securely keep credit cards on file and better PCI scores, although they don't have a chip reader. Hmmm … The card sliding device doesn't work with my laptop, though, and the "security" features like having to enter the house number and zip code with each transaction are turning into more of an annoyance. As you can tell, I'm not thrilled with it so far. We'll see how this goes. I might end up back with the mobile system. On the other hand, bank statements are a lot easier to balance since I don't have to do the mental math of deposit = charge – fees for each day.

    Why would you want to keep credit card numbers on file? I have a cancellation/no-show policy of $50 for the first late (<24 business hour) cancellation or no-show, what I would've gotten for a 90834 session for the second one, and $150 for the third and thereafter. As you can imagine, even though people agree to the policy on paper, sometimes they're not thrilled about paying it. Having a credit card on file allows us to collect the money for those fees and for balances owed. Of course someone from the office always lets the client know when their card is going to be charged before we run it.

Scheduling

Another reason to have the internet in your office is online scheduling. I do know some practitioners who still use paper calendars, and if you want to do that, I will not judge. As you can imagine, though, having an online scheduling system can make life so much easier. Here are a couple of examples as to how:

First, when you have an online schedule, you can adjust it and see it from anywhere, including your tablet or phone. Yes, this means your devices have to be password protected, and you have to be very careful with them. But they're a smidge more secure than a paper calendar, and I do like being able to make appointments and work around my schedule when I'm not at the office. Plus, if something does happen to my device, at least my schedule isn't totally lost. One thing to be aware of is that smartphones often have several calendars in them, so if you're making appointments remotely, you have to make sure they make it on to your office online calendar. I once double-booked myself with a doctor's appointment and an appointment at my office because the doctor's appointment went on to a different calendar. The easiest way I've found to do this is to make sure the appointment I'm making is categorized as the same color as the office appointments.

Second, if you decide to bring on administrative help, either real-life or virtual, it's much easier for two people to manipulate an online calendar than a paper one. It has occurred occasionally that my administrator has logged off before her calendar synchs, and we've double-booked appointments, but this is rare. It's also easier to share calendars, so if you and a colleague need to meet, you can check both calendars and propose times that are likely to work, which saves some back and forth.

Third, it makes for less work overall. The EHR calendar is also attached to an automated reminder system, and when I get my patient portal set up, people will be able to request appointments. Yes, I have an administrator for some of these tasks, but if she's out for some reason, it's nice to know reminders are still done. Plus, it frees up her time for other projects.

Whatever calendar system you use, I highly recommend having some redundancy. For example, right now I have a calendar in my EHR that's patient-only and an Outlook calendar for both patient and other appointments. There have been times—thankfully very rarely—that Enterprise, which hosts the Outlook calendar, has been down, so at least we've been able to make appointments in the EHR.

My Great Mistake

Sadly, being a mental health professional does not mean I get to avoid difficult people in the rest of my life. This is a cautionary tale about how not to lease an office space. It was difficult to tell what I did wrong when I was in the situation, but I've come to the conclusion that my great mistake in this situation was attacking the problem as a psychologist would, not as a businessperson. Remember how I said it's necessary to be able to shift back and forth? I failed at it in this case.

The first time I saw my current office space, it was a humid start to a sultry midsummer day in Atlanta. I'd voted in a runoff election and was sitting in the parking lot of a cute little office building I'd had my eye on. I'd talked to the leasing agent, who agreed to show a couple of spaces on the bottom floor to me and my colleague David, with whom I've gone into a space-sharing arrangement. "Be there at 8:15," the agent had written me. "The current tenants are on a very tight schedule." I got there at 8:12. David arrived at 8:15, and we chatted as we waited. And waited. And waited. Finally at 8:32—tight timeline, remember?—I called the real estate agent, who answered the phone and blustered, "I'm at the light. I'll be there in less than two minutes."

He was there in less than one, zipping into the drive, straight past us, and to the lower parking lot. Then he came back. Not bothering to get out of his car, he rolled down the window and told us he'd meet us in the back. When we arrived at the bottom of the slight hill, he showed us the spaces, starting with the one that wasn't on a tight schedule. He finished that tour by telling us we couldn't have it because they were "first come, first serve," and he'd already sort of promised it to someone else. That worked out because the other one was better for what David and I wanted to do. We agreed to pursue it, although neither of us were impressed with the agent.

Lesson number one—when someone rubs you the wrong way, listen to your gut. You will see that this is a theme.

The next stage of the game was negotiating the lease itself. This felt like a high-pressure situation because we were going for space in a highly desirable area, both with regard to location and demographics. I felt a time crunch since I had to give notice on my current space at the end of July, and I didn't feel comfortable doing so until I had another office lined up. The lease negotiation was more of the same with this individual, who had a very aggressive negotiation style, in my opinion.

Lesson number two—use your own commercial leasing agent or a business lawyer when negotiating a lease.

I'm regretting signing that lease, not because of the space, but because I feel I could've gotten a better deal and avoided some of those clauses you should look out for (see Boxes 2.1 and 4.1). Also, insurance companies—including the one I used—shy away from what they perceive as being a "roommate agreement," or two people sharing the same space and signing the lease separately. The agent insisted that I allow him to talk to my insurance agent. I have a really good relationship with the broker, having been with the company for years, and my psychologist self wanted to put a boundary in place between the leasing agent and the insurance agent so as not to damage that relationship. This resulted in me being labeled as "resistant."

Lesson number three—let businesspeople sort things out among themselves if it's appropriate. I should've trusted the broker to act on my behalf, which he did.

Lesson number four—get the landlord contact info from the beginning.

There's no reason that if someone's agent ends up being a jerk that you shouldn't be able to go to their boss. The agent withheld the landlord contact info until the insurance policy stuff was settled about a week and a half before move-in date. I needed the info for the business license process, which delayed me getting it, which added more stress.

Don't get me wrong, I'm very happy with the new space, but I suspect I could have been equally as happy with another space and saved myself the headache of dealing with that individual. I tried to brush off my feelings as not handling cultural differences well, and I ignored a lot of the red flags. Also, the property manager was cc'd on the bulk of the emails, so now that I've been labeled as "resistant," I have to let David make requests on our behalf. It kind of makes sense for him to do so since I'm technically subleasing from him to satisfy the insurance requirements, but I feel like I've lost some of my agency. As much as I hate moving, it's going to take some serious renegotiations with someone else for me to agree to renew that lease, which at the end of the day is the landlord's loss.

Conclusion and Action Steps

Now that you've been pondering space and gathering equipment, which has hopefully been fun for you, it's time to update those lists I had you start in the last section. You can put the amounts you spent on the worksheets or add to a spreadsheet, whatever works best for you. When I interviewed other therapists for this book, I asked them what the biggest challenge in starting a private practice was. Several of them told me that putting systems in place in order for the office itself to run smoothly was the hardest part. One way to start planning your office procedures may be to ponder what you want your clients' experience to be when they first call the office to make an appointment, when they come in to see you, and then when they schedule again. Everyone is going to do this differently, so I'm not going to tell you exactly what to do, only that the process needs to be as easy for you and your staff as it is for your clients.

One way to make the first contact better and to make sure everything is done legally and ethically is to have help. In the next chapter I'm going to talk about what and when to delegate to other professionals.

Box 3.1 Interview with the Expert: Weslee Knapp

Commercial real estate agent Weslee Knapp is the owner and broker at Keller-Knapp, Inc. He helped me to find my very first office space when I struck out on my own after leaving the group practice. He was kind enough to answer a few questions for me about the interesting and complicated world of commercial real estate (W. Knapp, personal communication, January 30, 2017).

What are some of the terms we see on leasing flyers, and what do they mean? For example, what are Class A, B, and C buildings, and what costs and amenities should we expect with each? Also, Expenses (e.g., 2014 tax at $0.58/SF), number of square feet "contig" to building and floor, direct vs. indirect type lease?

Good questions.

Class A—Think of this as your perfect home that is typically modernized and in a really good location.—You will always pay a premium

Class B—Think of this as something that at one point in time might have been a class A, but it has aged some or is not in a great location even if it is modernized. This is a better option than A if you do not need high-end space.

Class C—Think of this as something that has both aged quite a bit and is in a less than ideal location. This would typically be used if you are just opening an office.

For expenses, most people need to understand the term CAM or Common Area Maintenance, which would be what is specified as a tenant requirement as part of a lease/rental payment. Each tenant pays a percentage of the costs to maintain, or provide upkeep for, the areas that are outside of the individual offices and that everyone in the building uses such as hallways, lobbies, and bathrooms.

You have three types of leases.

Triple Net—Where you lease the spaces, but all expenses including insurance, taxes on the building, all utilities, HVAC, water heater, roof, etc. can all be on the tenant.

Modified Gross—Some of the expenses are and some of the expenses are not. Be sure to know exactly what is paid in a modified gross lease.

Gross—This is common for office buildings to include janitorial, utilities, and all fees. However, the CAM is usually variable, so you want to understand those costs.

Number of square feet contiguous to building and floor—Amount of square footage you're looking into leasing vs. how much is available. They want to know if you're looking at renting all or part of it.

Indirect means subleasing from another company, direct is from the landlord or leasing company.

What are the aspects that affect rent prices? What are some other things such as length of lease, involvement of agent, etc.?

The longer you sign a lease for the more concessions you will get from a landlord. Specify in the lease exactly how you are supposed to receive the space. Is the landlord doing any TI (tenant improvements), and what are those? Are they giving you money, and are you responsible for doing the work? If you are responsible for the improvements, what are the specifications you have to follow in hiring people? Often, you have to use their people or have them on an approval list.

On high-rise buildings, understand if the building wants your space whether you can be moved and are they paying for it. In other words, if you're in a 2,000 square foot space, and the guy next to you who is renting 15,000 wants to expand, the landlord can opt to move you out of your space to make the larger tenant happy. Make sure there is something in the lease indicating that they will help relocate you, either in the building or nearby.

What sort of research should someone do before approaching a leasing agent?

Determine whether you are going to hire a broker or not to help you find space. The hard thing with a one or two office space is that it is not very lucrative for a broker to assist. However, if it is your first time doing it, a real estate leasing broker can really help you through the process. The three things that are helpful before going out with a broker to look at space are having your business plan mostly complete, having an idea of how it relates to how much space you need, and understanding in your business plan where you need to be located. Also be open to the possibility your plan might change or need to be refined based on the space you find.

What should renters look out for, e.g., potential red flags?

Look out for high escalations in leases each year. Normal escalations range between 2–4 percent. Anything more would have to be a special circumstance.

What should potential renters do before agreeing to a space?

Have a true business plan going in that you can articulate to the building owner or leasing agent. Also, understand the total monthly costs. Are there utility costs? Are there janitorial costs?

What are the advantages of buying a space vs. leasing one?

Leasing works well as it is an expense. If you are in a large building, you can often renegotiate for larger space with little penalty, if any, if you are growing. In leasing you are more mobile. You can usually sublease if everything fails.

Buying is good for building equity if you know you are going to stay the same size and want to remain in that location. The long-term equity you can build up is nice, but you are less mobile and lose some ability to make changes to your business.

What sort of financial documents should potential renters have ready?

Typically, you will need any business and personal tax records. Additionally, they will give you a document to understand your personal financials, as well. Typically, this is called a personal financial statement.

What types of clauses should renters look out for in a rental contract?

The big question is whether you have to give a personal guaranty. Most leases will ask for a personal guaranty unless you have proven yourself in business for a long time. Sometimes you can negotiate the length of time which may not be the full time of the lease as the personal guaranty.

In your opinion, what is the biggest mistake or misconception that potential renters have?

That renting an office is like renting an apartment. In some ways it is; however, there are a lot more things to consider in having space for your business than when you're renting an apartment.

Bibliography

Building Owners and Managers Association International. (n.d.). Building class definitions. Retrieved from http://www.boma.org/research/pages/building-class-definitions.aspx.

U.S. Small Business Association Office of Entrepreneurial Management. (June 1999). Americans with Disabilities Act ADA Guide for Small Businesses [downloadable pdf pamphlet]. Retrieved from https://www.ada.gov/smbusgd.pdf.

Worksheet 1—Wish List Prioritizer

Remember that list of things I wish I had in an office? Here it is again, but with spaces for you to prioritize what you'd like. Rank them in order of appeal or importance with 1 being most important, 2 slightly less, and so on. This is a good thing to have on hand when you're talking to a leasing agent or looking at space:

____ Designated storage space.
____ Back entrance.
____ Climate control in the office.
____ Good soundproofing between offices and suites.
____ Mail delivery straight to and pickup directly from the office. Again, this may not be possible, but it never hurts to ask.
____ Internal hallway.
____ Ensuite bathroom.
____ Break room.
____ Receptionist area that can be closed off.

Worksheet 2—Office Setup Checklist

So you've chosen an office space? Great! Here's the checklist of things you need to do and set up:

1. Utilities
    ____ Phone—landline or VOIP? Do you have your phone system yet?
    ____ Internet—are the cables present?
    ____ Gas
    ____ Electric
    ____ Water
2. Furniture—therapy room
    ____ Therapist's chair
    ____ Patient's chair or couch
    ____ Desk
    ____ Desk chair
    ____ End tables
    ____ Lamps
    ____ Bookshelves
    ____ Decorations
3. Furniture—waiting room and administrator space
    ____ Chairs
    ____ End table
    ____ Lamp
    ____ Administrator desk, chair, computer, lamp, and phone—if applicable
    ____ Filing cabinets—make sure you can lock them
    ____ Decorations
4. Equipment
    ____ Computer
    ____ Printer
    ____ Fax machine or scanner
    ____ Monitor
    ____ Phone system

The Big Decisions

II

To Delegate or Not to Delegate

4

October 19, 2016—After seeing four patients, I took my new post-doc to lunch. Then I returned to the office, where I had a phone call with a compliance specialist who was helping me to get policies and procedures in place to maintain the integrity of the protected health information in my practice. After that, I met with two sales reps from my payroll company, one of them is on the Human Resources side and one helps companies set up 401k plans. Yes, they arrived together, so it was efficient. I'll talk more about those meetings later in the chapter.

Yes, the only income-generating activity I did that day was seeing those four patients, and on the surface, spending an hour talking to compliance consultants may seem like a waste of time. Once you start your business, however, you enter a world where the number of rules and regulations, as well as the chances to screw up, increase exponentially as you add more people to your practice. Even if your practice is only you, you still need to have certain policies in place. As attorney Linda Collett (see Box 2.1) likes to say, "You don't know what you don't know," and since she's a lawyer, I mentally add, "until it's too late." So, in this chapter, I'm going to talk about areas to consider outsourcing or delegating. Why? Because if you're spending time reading and trying to understand all the many laws that govern what you do and then writing the policies to satisfy them, you're not spending that time seeing patients or clients, which brings in revenue, and, I'm guessing, is what you would prefer to do.

Plus, you don't know what you don't know.

Administrative

When I first moved into my own office in 2010, I spent a week getting everything set up and organized, then opened my doors to patients. I already had a good referral stream from having started with a group practice, so I got busy quickly. I also learned that it's not easy to manage all the little office tasks and spend 6–7 hours a day seeing clients. Consequently, those tasks got pushed to the corners of the day, or I tried to sneak them in. In case you're wondering, if you're going to be assembling charts while on a conference call, it's best to put yourself on mute. Yeah, two-hole punches are not quiet, and I got busted. The tipping point came when I was finishing up at the office—making charts, filing, etc.—at 8:00 p.m. and my husband called and said, "You know, you should really hire someone. I'd like to see you sometime."

I'm stubborn, but I could see his point. Dealing with all the phone calls, filing, and other minutiae was keeping me at work too late and making me grumpy when I did get home because I felt perpetually behind. Plus, I couldn't keep up with filing. Okay, I hate filing. I had a billing service at the time, so at least I wasn't doing that, but I still needed to enter the checks and do all the accounting work.

So I hired my first part-time administrator for 15 hours a week. She came in the mornings, which is when the phones are busiest. Things ran so much more smoothly, and I was getting home by 6:00–7:00 p.m. Since then, I've come to be even more grateful for the help for more than just the office management pieces. This is also a good place for you to start with your admin job description. I've included mine at the back of this chapter.

First, how many hours a week do you want help? On the low end, if you're fine handling your phones or have gone to an online scheduling system and just need someone for filing and faxing notes to referral sources—yes, unfortunately the medical world still runs on fax machines—then consider hiring a psychology student from a local college to come in a few hours a week and dig you out from all that paper. They're cheap and will work as much for the experience and letter of recommendation as for the money. In the middle, which is what I do, you can have someone at 15–20 hours a week to take phone calls, do your filing and faxing, verify insurance benefits, get information from new patients (who require longer phone calls), and check patients in and out. On the upper end, you can hire someone full-time, but that seems to be a better arrangement for when you have more than one provider working in the office because otherwise there might not be enough work to justify an administrator being there for 40 hours a week. The practices I've seen who have someone full-time have at least two full-time providers.

How much do you pay your administrator? That depends on how much they do for you, of course. You can get a rough idea of the going rate from the U.S. Department of Labor Bureau of Labor Statistics site, but it returns earnings in terms of medians, which, as you hopefully remember from your stats class, isn't the average, but rather the middle number. When I looked at it today (in December 2016), administrative weekly earnings were $673–679 across the first three quarters of 2016, or almost $17/hour (U.S. Department of Labor Statistics, n.d.). In areas like mine, where cost of living is lower, hourly rate is less. Due to several factors, going rates for administrators vary by state and area, so I recommend you research this with your colleagues.

One of the intangible benefits of having an administrator is that they can serve as a buffer between you and the clients over potentially awkward rapport-damaging matters like money. Some people seem to equate mental health practitioners with nice people who don't need to get paid for their services or at the very least shouldn't talk about it. I actually had a client cancel an initial session because I was the one who did the intake phone call, which includes asking about insurance and getting a credit card to keep on file. She called back and told me she was offended that the doctor talked about money right away, and I should have someone do that for me. This is not a common complaint, especially since I'm now sure to tell people I prefer to run a no-surprises practice, but still.

Lesson learned—unless I'm trying to fill a slot the next day, I now let my admin make new patient appointments. We need to be able to talk about finances, but it's nice to have someone else be the bad guy. That's how medical practices do it.

Now that we're in the computer age, some practices are making use of virtual assistants. Obviously this is not going to get your filing done, but we do all our faxing directly from our Electronic Health Records (EHR) system or through an online faxing service, which can be done remotely. Virtual receptionists can take phone calls to make or change appointments, but they may not be able to answer questions about the finer points of your practice like someone in-house would because they're likely working for several providers. For example, when a new patient is lost, it's much easier for someone in the office familiar with the area to direct them. Another point about virtual assistants that we'll get to when we reach compliance—you need to have several layers of protection in place to ensure your client data is safe.

Billing

One of the best parts about having your own business is that you get to see exactly how the money comes in and where it goes. This can also be very time-consuming and frustrating, especially when you start dealing with insurance companies. When I started my practice, I was advised to use the billing service the other people in the group contracted with, and it went well, especially before I got really busy. They charged their fees based on what they brought in, so they were motivated to collect. This was a definite plus. On the other hand, the more money that came in, the higher the fees got. Yes, this was one of those necessary "spend money to make money" situations, but the fees still felt like a lot. Plus, since the service worked for several practices, they didn't necessarily follow up on things as quickly or persistently as I would have done myself.

There are two major advantages of having a billing service. The first is that, in addition to having an administrator, it's a way to avoid potential awkward financial conversations. Most of them, anyway. Even if you have someone taking money in the office and a billing service, you're still going to have to speak with some of your clients about money at some point. The other is that professional billers are trained and knowledgeable—or should be—about what sort of contact is necessary to get required pre-authorizations and address problems with insurance companies, and so they may be more effective than regular office staff. My previous billing person even sent a complaint to the state insurance commissioner after one insurance company refused to change my address after my first move. Whereas our appeals to the insurance company didn't get anything resolved, going to the insurance commissioner did. I would recommend this only as a last resort.

When I got my EHR system, I had the option to add billing to it and bring the process in-house. I waited a year so I could get used to the clinical side of it, and then I made the plunge. Most EHR systems have billing integrated with them now, and they've gotten very easy to use. When everything goes as it should, the process is smooth—you send in the information, and the insurance company sends you money. The tricky part comes in when claims are denied or just don't get processed for whatever reason, or if you're dealing with a client's insurance that requires pre-authorization for mental health benefits. That often requires someone to call the insurance company, but they, like many businesses, have moved pre-authorization requests and benefits information online. If you have office staff, they can do that for you and handle most of the problems. I do have one situation currently that will likely require me to call, but I only have to do so a couple of times a year. We also have a new policy in place that we will try twice to get the insurance company to pay for a visit, and if they deny it both times, the client is responsible.

One of my book interviewees recommended doing your own billing to start out with, but with that you risk getting behind. Although I'd had some experience dealing with insurance companies on behalf of an allied health professional when I worked for a chiropractor one summer, I learned a lot from having the billing service at first. Insurance companies have their own personalities, and I appreciated knowing their quirks when I moved my billing in-house.

Accounting and Bookkeeping

The most basic part of running a business is balancing the money coming in with the money that's going out. Some people are afraid of the numbers or don't feel they can handle managing the money once it gets a little more complicated. Don't judge yourself and get behind—that's what a bookkeeper is for.

At their most basic level of service, bookkeepers keep track of the money that comes in and the money that goes out. They pay bills, reconcile bank and credit card statements, and make sure the credit cards get paid. They'll also make deposits for you. According to Carly Berg of Above & Beyond Bookkeeping, they can also do more in-depth analysis and consultation to help businesses improve their profits.

While I'm comfortable handling my own bookkeeping—okay, I kind of enjoy it—taxes are beyond me. When I started my practice and taxes became more complicated than just entering numbers on lines, my husband and I decided to enlist the aid of an accountant. The tax code is quite complicated, and I didn't want to end up breaking laws I didn't know existed.

The first thing my accountant did was help me with incorporation. He explained the financial advantage of having a P.C. over an LLC, and he went through the process of setting the company up with the Secretary of State's office for me. At this point now that I know what I'm doing, I'm more inclined to set up any future corporations myself. At the beginning, when I felt overwhelmed by all the rules and regulations, it was nice to know that I didn't have to worry about it being done correctly.

The second thing my accountant did was encourage me to get QuickBooks to track my money. This is corporate accounting software, and I'll discuss it further in Chapter 6. Briefly, it helps me to keep track of charges, payments, and the money I spend, which is important for budgeting. It's also helpful because I can send an accountant's copy to him at tax time. There are other software packages such as Xero, but the one you use will likely depend on what your accountant wants you to use.

Third, my accountant set me up with a payroll company (see next section), which I had given him permission to contact. He has guided decisions such as setting myself up as a salaried employee of my company so taxes are withheld, and I don't have to personally pay them quarterly, which you have to do if you're not automatically having them done through your paycheck.

At this point, the only time I'm in contact with my accountant is during tax season and then during the year if other questions come up. It's very helpful that he also handles my personal taxes, so he has the whole picture. Could I do my corporate and personal taxes at this point? Maybe, but if I were to apply my hourly rate to the time I'd have to spend to learn how, it wouldn't make good financial sense. Plus, the tax code is quite complicated, and I know I'd miss stuff. When I asked Kelly Locklear of Small Business Solutions what she would say to someone who felt they didn't need to hire an accountant, she was speechless for a moment. She then noted that the only people she's known of who felt that way were the ones she then had to try to rescue when they were audited. Beyond being prepared for auditing, she identified the advantages of having an accountant as someone who is "on your side" when it comes to dealing with government agencies and who can best find all of the possible deductions.

From my perspective, it's been really nice to have someone "on call" to ask questions. I've been able to shoot my accountant a quick email when I'm pondering adding a new service or employee, or if I want to keep some money aside. For example, with the recent office move, I knew I would need to have more money in reserve, so my accountant helped me figure out what my salary and profit distributions should look like for the remainder of the year. He also helps me keep track of office property value, along with depreciation, or the lessening of value of office equipment and furniture over time. That's important to know for both insurance and tax reasons.

Payroll/HR

At some point, you'll get to start paying yourself. Yes, it might sound ominous that you don't get to do it immediately, but that's one reason you're reading this book—so you can save yourself time and money on the front end to help you get to that point sooner, or at least figure out when that may happen. When you do start giving yourself a paycheck, you'll need to subtract taxes and send those in to the government quarterly. How much do you subtract? How do you make sure you remember to send it in? And how do you make sure it gets to the right place?

That's where a payroll company comes in. I've got my payroll set up so that salaried and hourly employees like me and my office manager get paid twice a month, and my contractors are paid once a month. About a week before each payday, the payroll company emails me a reminder, and I let them know what my base salary will be, how many hours the office manager has worked, and, if applicable, what the contractor will be paid. They issue the direct deposits and take the money from my checking account for the payments, the taxes, and their fees. They email me when my payroll report is ready, and I go into their system, download it and the pay stubs, and enter it all into QuickBooks. They send the taxes into the government quarterly for me, let me know when they do, and send me reference copies. At the end of the year, they send me 1099s and W-2s for my employees and give me those reference copies to give my accountant.

With the payroll company on board, paying myself and my employees is an easy process that takes me about fifteen minutes total twice a month, much less time than if I were doing all the calculations and payment issuing myself. Kelly Locklear of Small Business Solutions recommended that businesses always outsource payroll because of time savings. She also mentioned that, like accounting, it's another area with a vast amount of knowledge, particularly with regard to taxes, that business owners can get into trouble for not knowing.

Other areas payroll companies are helpful are with human resources requirements and retirement. With regard to human resources, when you have employees, you have a certain number of (surprise!) government requirements such as signage, manuals, and, as we've discussed, payroll itself. Some payroll companies will offer assessments to ensure businesses meet the minimum requirements in case of audit.

Paychex HR specialist Martin Joseph Manigross visited my practice to pitch Paychex's HR services. He informed me that human resources laws are constantly changing, nuanced, and multi-layered, so it's difficult for the average business owner to stay on top of them. According to Manigross, the most common mistake businesses make, and are penalized for, is employee classification, specifically classifying employees who should get a W-2 at the end of the year as contractors, or 1099 employees. Why? Remember, taxes get withheld from the W-2 employee's paycheck and paid by the company, so the government gets more taxes for the non-contractors (J. Manigross, personal communication, October 19, 2016).

A human resources specialist can ensure that businesses are meeting requirements so that contractors are, indeed, contract employees. For example, while hourly and salaried employees don't set their own hours, contractors do. Contract employees also use their own equipment. HR specialists can also ensure that businesses have the proper manuals and paperwork for their employees.

It seems that it shouldn't be too hard to figure out whether your employees are contractors or regular employees, but when I went to look on the IRS website on the topic, I found this paragraph:

> Businesses must weigh all these factors when determining whether a worker is an employee or independent contractor. Some factors may indicate that the worker is an employee, while other factors indicate that the worker is an independent contractor. There is no "magic" or set number of factors that "makes" the worker an employee or an independent contractor, and no one factor stands alone in making this determination. Also, factors which are relevant in one situation may not be relevant in another.
>
> (Internal Revenue Service, 2016)

As with many things having to do with the government, that explanation ends up being less clear than would be ideal.

Another area a payroll company can help is with retirement and benefits, both for you and employees to help attract and retain them. They often have relationships with others in the area and can coordinate payments to be taken out of paychecks. Some types of retirement plans can actually save businesses money because the money is taken out pre-tax.

After-Hours Coverage

It's a common assumption in the profession that we need to be on call 24/7 for our clients. When I started my practice, I was in a group situation, so it didn't seem too bad. The group contracted with an after-hours service, so the responsibility could be shared. It was possible to be "not on call," for example, while on vacation because there were others who were able to cover for us.

Once I moved into my own office and had my own practice, I started doing all my own after-hours calls. I quickly recognized that being on call all the time was exhausting, even though I only got called twice in the five and a half years I was doing it. I wondered why I was feeling so burned out, and I realized that aside from the periods when I had another psychologist working with me and was able to trade off call, I hadn't been able to completely relax.

No matter how unlikely a crisis is to happen, the mind is geared to expect it and prepares for it on some level. Then there were times I traveled and was out of touch for several hours, either due to being in airplanes, being out of the country, or being in conference centers with poor cell signal. Also—and this is my personal feeling—it's not fair to expect a professional in any situation to be perpetually available. We need our life / work balance and family harmony, too. Once I bring on more psychologists, I'll be able to go back to running after-hours calls through the practice, but at this point, I've found a solution that works for me, which is to not take after-hours calls.

That said, if a client reaches out after-hours, there needs to be some sort of resource for them. Here are some options:

Answering Service

This is the most expensive option. The way this typically works is that after-hours calls to a practice are routed to an answering service, which will call—it used to be page—the doctor, who then calls the patient back. This works best in situations where there's more than one doctor in a practice, and patients are trying to reach their own provider, but there's only one number to do so. The answering service can also be instructed as to who has the backup calls for that period of time. For example, in my first situation, we all took turns taking backup calls for a week. That meant that if one doctor wasn't available, there was still someone to talk to the patient. It worked beautifully except for when the psychiatrists' patients called for emergency refills, which of course the non-M.D.'s couldn't help with.

After-Hours Line

This is a number that patients can call after-hours that forwards to your personal cell phone. As I mentioned before, I was using Google Voice for this, but there were some issues. For example, there's still a question of whether Google will sign a business associate agreement (see next section). If I want to return to using an after-hours line, which I might once I bring on more providers to share call, my VOIP system has an option.

Crisis Hotline/911/Emergency Room

The only reason a patient should need to talk to you after-hours is if they're considering harming themselves or someone else. Several providers I know will advise clients to call 911 or proceed to the nearest emergency room and ask for a psych evaluation. Since going to an ER can be intimidating, I try to direct my patients to a mental-health-focused resource. In my outgoing voicemail, I give the number for a local crisis hotline.

I asked some of the providers I interviewed what they did for after-hours calls, and almost all of them, like me, don't do it. Many of them came up with a compromise, for example, giving their cell phone numbers only to particular clients or said they would only be on call until a certain time (e.g., 8:00 p.m.). Others said clients could call, and the provider said they would try to get back to them, but they didn't promise immediate responses. A few told me they deliberately did not work with patients who would be likely to call after hours. Again, this is your decision, but as we'll talk about later, this is a good time for you to start thinking of your own balance and self-care.

Compliance

Whenever I hear the word "compliance," I'm tempted to think of a whip-wielding bureaucrat standing over a hapless businessperson, who is cowering and covering his or her head. I might even sometimes refer to compliance as the "c-word." Yes, a lot of this feels like busy work, which is why it can be helpful to delegate it to someone else.

I first learned about HIPAA (Health Insurance Portability and Accountability Act) compliance when I was in graduate school. It seems that a lot of it can be summed up in one sentence—don't be stupid when it comes to patient information—but of course it's way more complicated, and just like HR laws, the HIPAA/HITECH (Health Information Technology for Economic and Clinical Health) laws have a lot of layers and change frequently. The type of information that's most at risk, and therefore most protected, is designated as PHI or Protected Health Information. This includes identifying information about the patients, what they're coming to you for, and what happens in session. I've been working with a HIPAA and HITECH compliance company on getting "buttoned up," as consultants like to say. The first thing they had me do was to get a set of policies. Are you ready to start keeping count? That's two sets if you separate HIPAA and HITECH, three if you count the ones you give to your patients as a separate set.

Beyond policies, which apply to the environment you hopefully have control over, there are rules governing people who have access to your client information. These could include but aren't limited to:

- Electronic Health Records (EHR) vendors
- Insurance filing sites
- Shredding companies
- Telemental health platforms
- Email, calendar, and other office software or sites

Whenever someone has access to PHI, my compliance company puts them through a due diligence process, wherein they ask them a bunch of questions, and have them sign a Business Associate Agreement (BAA). You can see why I farm this out—I don't have time to chase people for due diligence and BAAs. The company has also been invaluable in helping me to find a good EHR and with other tech stuff. For example, they have discount agreements with certain vendors, and they were able to point me to a contractor who gave me a very reasonable quote on running the Ethernet cables. Finally, since interruption of care puts patients at risk, compliance consultants can help practices put in place a plan for if something catastrophic happens.

Working with Kardon has given me a much better sense of situations that may put my patients' PHI at risk. Most recently, we shifted our closed patient files to a HIPAA-compliant cloud-based server, which left us with a lot of boxes of paper that needed shredding. Shredding companies sometimes send postcards to my office with offers for services. Karla, my Kardon contact, had a list of ones that have completed, or are in the process of completing, due diligence interviews and BAAs. My previous office offered shredding days, and after working with Karla, I ensured that the PHI was in my hands or at least in sight (with people helping me carry boxes) between the office and when it got dumped in the onsite shredder. I would've been careful before, but it helped to have a framework and rationale for why I had to be so cautious.

You can read more about compliance in Box 4.1.

Box 4.1 Interview with the Expert: Donna Grindle

Thank you to Donna Grindle of Kardon Compliance for answering my questions! I've been working with Donna, Karla, and the Kardon team for years, and they've been very helpful. It's also comforting to know I'm doing everything I can to keep my patient information secure (D. Grindle, personal communication, January 5, 2017).

How would you define PHI?

PHI is defined in the HIPAA law as protected health information. Any data element that can be used to identify an individual connected to any healthcare information can be considered PHI. There are 18 identifiers that make a set of data considered as PHI. Some identifiers are obvious (patient name, social security number, medical record number) but others are not as obvious such as vehicle identification number which can be tracked to a patient.

How do practices put their PHI most at risk?

Most practices do not know all the locations that their PHI is created, received, stored or transmitted. That includes desktops, laptops, copier machines, printers, tablets, storage facilities, backup media, etc. Many people don't even realize they have PHI in their downloads folder in a spreadsheet or PDF. If you don't know where it is you can't protect it.

What are the minimum actions a practice needs to take with regard to HIPAA and HITECH compliance?

Perform a Security Risk Analysis (SRA) which is not just a short check-list or spreadsheet. There are free tools available from the Office of the National Coordinator for Health Information Technology to assist you in performing an SRA. However, many practices don't have someone who understands the technical questions the tool is asking you to evaluate. To perform a complete and thorough SRA, as required under HIPAA & MACRA (the Medicare Access and CHIP Reauthorization Act), you will need to get up to speed on your own technology.

Train your entire staff regularly on security and privacy, not just once a year.

Make privacy and security part of your day-to-day operations not a once a year task.

Encrypt all of your devices, especially any device that can move around easily.

What precautions should be taken when PHI is going to be shared with another practice or company? What are some situations that practices commonly miss?

Send only the minimum information necessary to meet the needs of the other practice in the care of this patient. If an entire medical record is not required for a case, then don't send the whole record.

Send the information securely via your EHR, encrypted email or secure fax.

The most common issues are sending more than the minimum necessary or not sending the information using a secure method. Sending records via standard email is not acceptable.

What minimum features should an EHR system have, both with regard to security and being able to start doing business again after a disaster?

The easiest way to know that an EHR has the minimum features is to see if it ever was classified as a Certified Electronic Health Record Technology (CEHRT). The first phase of meaningful use included most of the required security elements. All the systems that qualified for that version did not qualify for later stages.

If an EHR isn't CEHRT then you must confirm it has the ability to do the following within it (or any application that stores PHI):

Assign access to users based on their job role. Everyone doesn't need access to everything. Every user must use a unique user name at all times.

Require passwords to be complex and changed on a regular basis.

Set auto logout time periods that make sure any session is closed if you stop using it for a period of time.

Log user activity within the application and maintain that log for at least 6 years.

How frequently do EHR data breaches occur?

Every single day there is likely several healthcare data breaches somewhere in the U.S. In 2016, there was almost one every day that involved over 500 patients! Also in 2016, there were over 300 breaches reported to HHS that involved over 500 patients. The number of breaches involving less than 500 patients are dramatically higher than 300 and well into the thousands but they aren't reported in the same manner as larger ones.

Where can a professional go for good compliance information that's not written in legalese or some other secret language?

Often, associations that practices belong to have good resources on HIPAA and specifics regarding your specialty. Help Me with HIPAA (HelpMeWithHIPAA.com) is a weekly podcast that offers free training on privacy, security and breach rule information in a humorous, light format. Podcasts can be listened to on iTunes, Google Play, CastBox, at the computer and in numerous other ways. The HealthIT.gov offers training on security and privacy via interactive videos and even games at https://www.healthit.gov/providers-professionals/ehr-privacy-security.

What are the advantages of hiring a compliance company?

Privacy and security threats are constantly changing. These changes require refined guidance from the industry experts as well as the Department of Health and Human Services Office for Civil Rights. Compliance professionals spend all their time keeping up with this and understanding the often intricate nuances of privacy laws. Unless you have the time and expertise to understand all of these things yourself you will face an uphill battle. Seek out a compliance partner, not just someone who comes in and does a report for you. Most people don't understand what the report means and what it tells them they should be doing. Failure to meet your obligations to protect your patient's privacy can be devastating to them as well as you and your business.

Electronic Health Records

Like it or not, electronic health records are here to stay. They have several advantages as well as some disadvantages, but it's important to be aware that eventually—and this may be sooner rather than later—they may be required.

For me, the biggest advantage to having an electronic health records (EHR) system is efficiency. Prior to this system, I would write notes during session and then either type them out or use a template for my office note. New patient intake reports would take me about 10–15 minutes, and office notes 5–10 depending on their complexity, and even with templates, I found myself typing the same thing over and over. Very frustrating. Now, I have my EHR open on my iPad on my lap and type as I go. It doesn't end up being a lot, and the tablet is small enough that it doesn't interfere with patient/therapist rapport. At the end of session I clean up my notes, which only takes me a couple of minutes. Rather than taking away from quality of patient care, doing most of the notes during session adds to it because it gives me the flexibility to spend a few extra minutes with them if I need to. Since these notes are generated in the virtual chart, they don't need to be filed.

I didn't realize until I was talking to a colleague that not everyone can do their notes during session. He described it as not being able to listen, process, and type at the same time. However, he has also found that having an EHR has cut down his report-writing time significantly due to the use of templates. Many therapists use structured interviews, so we end up gathering the same type of information each time. Even if you don't like using report templates, consider where you end up writing the same thing repeatedly and think about how much time you could save. Bonus—referral sources tell me they like how clear and concise my notes are.

Another advantage to using an EHR is that it saves office space. Charts take up a lot of room. A colleague with whom I'm sharing the office is completely paperless—he scans and shreds things almost as soon as he gets them. I have paper charts for active patients that get shredded once the file is closed (more about closing files in the ethics section), but which don't include notes, which are only in the EHR. It's also more environmentally friendly.

Remember when I talked in the previous section about how part of compliance is risk management? I had a colleague here in Atlanta who did neuropsychological testing, and one year we had an autumn where it seemed like it had rained for the Biblical forty days and forty nights. Like many cities, we have a river with tributary streams, and my colleague lost everything—client charts and neuropsychological testing equipment—to a flood. Ouch, right? More recently, forest fires destroyed areas in and around Gatlinburg, Tennessee with very little warning, and I suspect many providers who didn't have electronic health records lost all their notes and charts.

Natural disasters and other catastrophes happen. Having files stored in the cloud with a service that is encrypted for security, but also backs them up so you can get to them from anywhere, is a smart move and an ethical one as you can pick up with client care once you find a new location.

EHR systems can also help to streamline general office tasks. For example, if you choose to file insurance, most EHR systems have that integrated now along with accounts receivable capabilities, so you can track patient balances and payments inside them. They also provide a nice backup system for scheduling, or a primary one if you choose to keep a backup calendar elsewhere.

That said, there are a few disadvantages to having electronic health records. One major issue is that if the internet goes down at your office site, you don't have access to your notes. One way around this may be to print out the most recent one and just keep one in the chart, or to keep a full paper chart for your active clients. Another disadvantage is that they're only as secure as your security policies, which is another reason it's good to have someone advise you on what to do. For example, compliance laws require that passwords be complex and changed every 90 days.

Just as with an ideal office space, I encourage you to come up with a wish list for what you want in an EHR. Scheduling and documentation are the basics. Insurance billing, especially if it's done automatically, can also be convenient and a huge time saver. One feature to consider is a patient portal, which allows patients to contact you electronically between sessions, but more securely than through email and more flexibly time-wise than with phone calls. Finally, the ability to fax notes to referring or consulting providers directly from the EHR also saves time.

Conclusion

One of my beta readers responded that she agreed that practices need accountants, but how do you find a good one? The best resource here is word-of-mouth, specifically from your fellow therapists. If you're new to an area, this is also a good reason to reach out to professional list-servs.

In the next chapter I'll emphasize the importance of niche specialization and how that fosters confidence in potential clients and leads to more referrals. The same process applies to us hiring other professionals. I wouldn't hire an accountant, billing service, or payroll company who'd never worked with a small private practice before. In fact, I'll talk in a future chapter about how I made a mistake hiring a marketing professional who had only worked with medical groups. Just as in therapy, it's important to find someone with whom you're a good "fit." It's always a good idea to interview before committing, and you definitely want to be comfortable handing over your company information.

If you're balking at the idea of farming out services, I get it. I'm somewhat stubborn, and unless it's something I know absolutely nothing about, I like to try to do something before hiring someone else. Remember, though—not only do you not know what you don't know, but you're not making the most efficient use of your time if you're spending hours on the internet trying to find the right set of policies or figure out your taxes. Ponder what your hourly rate is and see if the money balances out before deciding to do everything yourself. Also consider how expensive it could be if you get it wrong.

Another way to think about the ideas in this chapter is that you need to save not only your time, but your emotional energy, for your clients and have enough left at the end of the day for your family. What can you delegate to help you remain sane, peaceful, and balanced?

Bibliography

Internal Revenue Service. (November 28, 2016). Independent Contractor (Self-Employed) or Employee? Retrieved from https://www.irs.gov/businesses/small-businesses-self-employed/independent-contractor-self-employed-or-employee.

U.S. Department of Labor Statistics. (n.d.). Databases, Tables & Calculators by Subject. Retrieved from https://www.bls.gov/data/#wages.

Worksheet—Basic Administrative Job Duties

Patient interaction

Answer telephones
Make reminder calls
Check voicemails—main and doctors'
Schedule patients using Outlook
Check in new patients (see below)
Collect copays

General Office

Build charts
Filing
Copying
Notify Dr. B when office and/or coffee supplies are running low

Special Projects

Compile referral list
Patient file closing letters

New Patients

Scheduling
No more than 2 per day, 6 per week
Get phone, address, and mark as NEW (categorize red) on schedule

In Office
Copies of driver's license and insurance card
Paperwork—administer or collect if already filled out
Administer first session screening questionnaires; bring to doctor when
   completed

Daily Checklist

Reminder calls/emails 2 business days ahead

Faxing and filing of notes

Check voicemails and return calls or give messages to doctors

Day sheet for following patient day (list of patient, chart numbers, and amount they'll owe)

Special projects (patient closing letters, etc.)

Finding Your Niche   **5**

When you're setting yourself up as a private practitioner, it can be tempting to bill yourself as a generalist, or someone who handles all problems in all populations, or at least a lot of them. However, as you've probably figured out, psychology (or medicine, or chiropractic) is a broad area. Think about if you were to look for a therapist or other provider for a specific problem. You'd want to know that they not only have *expertise* but also *experience* in that area. From my conversations with other providers, I've found that they like to refer to specialists rather than generalists. I know I do.

Now that I've been practicing for over a decade, I've come to appreciate how I've grown not only as a therapist, but also as a behavioral sleep medicine specialist. Focusing on the same problem on an almost daily basis has helped me come to appreciate the nuances. I used to wonder what it meant to be an "experienced therapist," but then I reached a point where I recognized I didn't have to be anxious when faced with an unusual or tough case because I had seen something similar before. There's also something to being able to tell patients that you've helped lots of people with problems just like theirs, and no, they're not the worst case of _____ you've ever seen.

Side note, I've often wondered what someone would do if I told them that, yes, they are the worst case of insomnia I've ever seen. At this point I've seen so many, I couldn't honestly ask that question, and it would be mean to do so, so I haven't.

Another way to think of going general vs. niche is that one reason you're going into private practice is so you can have more control over your work and independence doing it. We all have types of patients we prefer not to see and ones we look forward to. While it's not necessary to love your job all the time, it's good to really like it most of the time. Focusing on treating the types of clients you enjoy the most is a good way to ensure you continue to be happy and satisfied with what you're doing.

You can probably tell I'm a big fan of specializing and setting up a niche practice. When you're doing so, consider which populations you most enjoy working with and which you don't. Brainstorm and get as specific as you like. For example, I like working with Type A personalities and overachievers. I knew from the beginning that I didn't want to work with kids because I didn't really want to work with parents. I also like manualized treatment and being able to make a big difference for someone in a short amount of time. When I was introduced to the field of behavioral sleep medicine, I knew I'd found my niche because the treatments are time-limited, the patients are often anxious Type A types, and there's more than enough demand for treatment of adult insomnia. And there's nothing more rewarding for me than helping someone sleep because it often means I'm giving them back their life.

Another way to approach finding your specialty is to think about what disorders most intrigue you. Did you have specialized training in something in graduate school, or did something you encountered on an internship or post-doc fascinate you so much that you had to learn all you could about it? Or does something click for you in a way you can't explain? Sometimes practitioners go into a specialty because they've overcome that particular problem and can bring a helpful perspective that gives hope to those who are still struggling. I had a patient who was thrilled to find a therapist who had overcome the same subtype of OCD he'd been dealing with because he knew she would understand his experience. If that's your situation, of course you want to make sure you've been stable for a while and know your signs and triggers for relapse.

I've had the opportunity to interview therapists in many different specialties, and it's been fun and fascinating to see how they landed where they are. In this chapter, I'll share some of their perspectives, but I'd like to start with mine.

How I Found My Niche

People choose their specialty based on different factors. As I mentioned, some have personally experienced the disorder they now treat. Some connected with their specialty through a practicum or internship experience. Some knew from the beginning what they wanted to do. And some came to their specialty through a series of fortuitous events. That's what happened to me, although at the beginning, I didn't see the circumstances as fortuitous at all.

In my graduate program, there was an expectation that certain milestones would be met at certain times, which meant we had strong cohorts. There was an expectation that the group you came in with was the group you'd finish with, and so setbacks were devastating, especially for those of us Type A overachievers, who tend to be the ones who go into higher education. Does this sound familiar? When I applied for internship, I did so as what I thought I wanted to be—an alcohol researcher and clinician focused on addictions.

Well, dear readers, I didn't match that year. Apparently I'd convinced myself that alcohol research was where I wanted to be, but no one else bought it. The rest of that spring semester was devastating—I'm pretty sure I went into a major depressive episode—and then in the summer I decided to try and expand my practicum experience so I'd be a better internship candidate the next go-round. I emailed graduates of my program who were in the Atlanta area, and one who responded was Michael Breus, a psychologist working in a sleep disorders, pulmonary, and critical care practice. We got along well, I found the work fascinating, and I ended up matching as a health psychology intern when I applied for internship again.

In spite of there not being a sleep medicine experience at the Central Arkansas VA internship site, one found me. When I was ready to go on my second rotation, my upcoming supervisor cornered me in the secretary's office. He was a short man with slicked-down black hair and a tiny mustache, so he wasn't that intimidating, but his message was.

"I have a message for you from God," he said. I should mention he had an interesting sense of humor.

My jaw dropped. "Really, Dr. K.? From God?"

"Yes. God told me he wants you to go to the director of the sleep medicine clinic and tell him you want to work with him while you're on my rotation."

I was no longer amused. The director of the sleep clinic was a dour pulmonologist, also with a mustache, and I didn't know how he would respond. But I took my little intern self up there and asked him, and he said yes. He actually ended up being a really nice guy once I got to know him. The last I heard, the internship still has a behavioral sleep medicine experience.

I had found my passion and my path. When I graduated, I eschewed the traditional post-doc path and went straight into Michael Breus's old job since he'd moved to the West Coast. Then when my contract was up, I had an opportunity to join that first practice, where I went into a space-sharing arrangement and had sleep study interpretation contract work to support me as I built my own client load.

So if you're still confused about your specialty, think about things that have happened in your training path. Have circumstances steered you toward a certain area? I'm not saying you've been given anything as obvious as a mission from God, but hey, if the universe has been that direct with you, that's great.

For the rest of you who are still pondering, let's talk about how some others have approached finding their niche. As you'll see, your niche can be as narrow and specific as you like.

By Population

One of the first questions to consider in training is what age group do you want to work with? When I went to graduate school, we had already sorted ourselves into the child people and the adult people. Private practice is much the same, but instead of two very broad populations, you can get as specific as you like with regard to age group.

As we go through our lives, the problems we face change. If you can position yourself as an expert in helping people with those problems, you will likely find the referrals flowing in.

Sometimes you may not find your passion while you're in graduate school or on internship. Geriatric psychologist Daniel Wachtel, Psy.D. worked as a case manager in a nursing home when he graduated from college. When I asked him what he liked best about working with this population, he told me, "It feels very rewarding. I'm working with clients who are going through some of the most challenging times in their lives. It feels good to work with a population that is often neglected and underserved by society. I also find that I continue to learn, and am continuously challenged, about life, aging, and end of life every day" (D. Wachtel, personal communication, December 14, 2016).

On the other end of the spectrum, child psychologists treat a different set of problems, as do those who work with adolescents. If you like working with systems as well as people, this may be an area for you. The child practitioners I interviewed talked about how they liked coordinating with families. They had both decided to go into child psychology in graduate school (A. Corbett, personal communication, January 18, 2017; K. Spencer, personal communication, January 18, 2017). Also, working with adolescents does take a certain patience, although it can be fun to see the seeds of what they'll turn into once they grow up a little. If this direction appeals to you but you weren't trained as a child psychologist, consider approaching a local child psychologist for mentoring and training or think about other areas where you could work with young people within systems.

You can get as specific as you like within age groups, even non-geriatric adults. For example, I recently came across a practice in my area of town that focuses on millennials. When I asked Dr. Debra Dantzler why she liked working with this very specific population, she said she enjoys helping those who are "struggling with questions of, 'How do I become my own adult person?'" (D. Dantzler, personal communication, January 6, 2017).

By Disorder or Treatment

When we think of niche specialization, the first thing that often comes to mind is treating specific disorders. This may initially seem like a way to pigeonhole yourself into doing the same thing over and over, but as we know, psychopathology is complex, and often people have more than one diagnosis. For example, I primarily treat insomnia at my practice, but the primary insomniac is so rare that the distinction between primary and secondary insomnia has been removed from the International Classification of Sleep Disorders and the DSM-5. I was in favor of this change because you do the same thing for both of them, cognitive-behavioral treatment for insomnia (CBTI), which has been demonstrated to work for insomnia on its own as well as that which developed as a result of something else, whether that other disorder was an illness (e.g., cancer), other medical issue (e.g., pain, menopause) or situation (e.g., birth of a child).

The thing that attracted me most to CBTI was that it works in a short amount of time. Sometimes I have to remind myself of this after second sessions, when many people have seen progress, but often the tough cases haven't. This is also the appeal for those who specialize in treating different types of anxiety disorders.

As you can see, often disorders become paired with specific types of therapy. As in my case and those of several of the practitioners I interviewed, a certain therapeutic modality has been found to be the most effective, and becoming an expert in that modality is rewarding. While there is such a thing as therapeutic skill, it's immensely helpful—and, let's be honest, easier—to be doing something that has been shown to work repeatedly. As my colleague Joshua Spitalnick, PhD, noted about exposure therapy and cognitive-behavioral treatment for anxiety, "In a soft science field, I wanted something with science, evidence, and that has been proven" (J. Spitalnick, personal communication, January 13, 2017).

Sometimes therapists find this direction through personal experience. For example, Shala Nicely, a Licensed Professional Counselor, suffered from OCD for most of her life before finally encountering Exposure and Response Prevention therapy. She saw there was a great need for it and went back to school so she could start helping others with similar problems to what she'd overcome (S. Nicely, personal communication, November 4, 2016). She's the therapist my one client was so relieved to find.

It's possible to specialize within specialty. For example, Pegah Moghaddam, PhD, who started with a specialty in eating disorders and branched into PTSD, told me she had been interested in eating disorders before she went into psychology. Then she specialized further when she discovered the sub-populations she liked most were those who also needed trauma work (P. Moghaddam, personal communication, August 24, 2016).

By Very Specific Niche

At this point if you don't have a clear specialty in mind, that's okay. Sometimes it occurs organically once you've started and have figured out what populations are accessible and what type of client you prefer to work with. Many providers have found themselves in a niche they didn't anticipate, but they enjoy where they ended up.

I recently had the pleasure of meeting Bill Herring, LCSW. He has the most specific niche I've encountered yet. As he wrote to me, "I help people who are struggling with aspects of their sexual behavior or that violate their relationship commitments, run counter to other important values, and/or exceed the limits of their perceived self-control." In other words, he works with unfaithful partners and those who are hurt by them. As you can imagine, he does a lot of couples' work (B. Herring, personal communication, January 23, 2017).

Debra Dantzler, whom I've already mentioned, also has a very specific specialty. Within the millennial age group, she tends to work with the LGBTQ population. Since she's fascinated by questions of identity and likes helping young people navigate difficult paths and "becoming their own adult person," this is a great niche for her (D. Dantzler, personal communication, January 6, 2017).

Both these providers came to their specialties through a gradual narrowing of focus. In Herring's case, he narrowed from working with adults and children to adults only to adults only with "personal struggles that sensitized me to the intricacies of these issues," to seeking more training and opportunities. Eventually he became the person known for this sort of work. Dantzler also started more broadly, but due to her connections in college counseling centers, found a specific client population she connected with. Both are emerging areas, which makes them particularly exciting.

Conclusion

If you're pondering starting a private practice, you may have already decided on your niche. If you're still thinking you'll start as a generalist, I encourage you to at least pick a broad area within psychology and mental health to focus on. For example, you may start narrowing by choosing mood disorders or anxiety disorders and then allow your patient population and referrals to guide you as to further specification. Whatever area you choose, make sure it's something you'll be happy doing for many years to come. This is your practice—there's no reason for you to suffer more than you need to, and sometimes doing fulfilling work is what will keep you going when the details of the business frustrate you.

One potentially frustrating part of running a business is dealing with money, which is what we'll focus on in the next chapter.

Worksheet—Finding Your Niche

I'm assuming at this point that you've been seeing clients somewhere, so you hopefully have an idea of what you enjoy and don't about the profession. Let's go through some questions to help you determine what your specialty might be if you haven't figured it out already. Even if you have figured out what you want to do, think within that population about what kind of patients you want to attract. Doing so will help you when we start talking marketing strategy. This isn't meant to be a life-directing quiz, by the way, but just some questions to help you clarify your thinking about what you want to do.

1. Think about your favorite client, either current or past. Describe them in writing or to yourself.

2. What did you like most about working with them? Was it the nature of their problem? Their personality? Their stage of life? The way they responded to treatment?

3. Now think about a different client, one that made an impression on you for another positive reason. Answer #2 for that person, too.

4. Ponder someone you didn't like working with. What turned you off about them?

5. While thinking about the clients you enjoyed, put together a statement like, "I really want to work with more people who are _____, _____, _____, and _____."

6. While recalling the person you didn't like, assemble a statement with, "I don't enjoy working with clients who are _____, _____, _____, or _____."

7. Complete the following statement: My favorite kind of therapy to do is _____.

8. Complete the following statement: The kind of therapy I least enjoy is _____.

9. Complete the following statement: My biggest strength as a therapist is _____.

10. Now imagine you've been in private practice for a year. What is one type of patient you can imagine seeing or therapy you could imagine doing and never get tired of? What is a disorder or distress-provoking situation that you will always find fascinating? Another way to think about this question might be, when you see continuing education opportunities, which ones appeal to you most?

11. Think about your mission statement. What clients or therapeutic approach will best help you fulfill it? Is there a need you perceive that you can fill, for example, a type of therapy or treatment that appeals to you but where there's a lack of providers?

Now do some free writing with the answers to the above questions in mind. What kind of client will you be happy about seeing on your schedule? What kind of work will help you feel fulfilled as a therapist? That's probably the direction you should go in.

Money Talks—How Well Do You Listen? **6**

Money can be an uncomfortable topic, especially if you're going into private practice from a hospital or other setting where financial transactions were handled by someone else far removed from you. I recently had lunch with a fellow allied health provider, who had come from a hospital setting and said the services she provided were treated as "being for the common good." Consequently, because she hadn't had to take payments and because her services had been labeled as more altruistic than profit-generating, she felt very anxious when she started seeing clients. She dreaded the end of sessions, when she had to ask for a credit card or other form of payment. As I mentioned in a previous chapter, I've encountered patients who weren't comfortable with the provider being involved in finances. Unfortunately, being in private practice requires handling money, both collections and what you spend for the business.

Setting Your Rates

I saw some advice in an email newsletter to talk to other psychologists about their rates when you're trying to determine yours. One thing to be aware of when talking to others in our field about sessions fees is that psychologists are considered to be economic competitors with each other, and therefore we fall under antitrust laws. Basically, that means that we can't legally discuss the fees we charge clients with each other because it's considered price fixing. This was a much bigger issue for new practitioners, who had no other way of knowing the "market rate" for the area, prior to the advent of the internet and practice websites. That's one reason it's advantageous to start off in a group or space-sharing arrangement, where you're sharing, not competing for, referrals. So, to clarify, the other providers and I can discuss our rates in my practice, but I can't do so with the psychologist across the street even though he's a couples' therapist, and we're more likely to cross-refer than compete.

Sometimes a state association may have data on fees collected under a "safe harbor" procedure. The data will be a few years old, but it may be a place to start. Another place to consider looking is at the Medicare fee schedule, which is available online, and use that as a starting point. A low starting point. Again, remember, the internet is your friend here.

So how do you set your fees? Let's say you can get an idea of what the market rate in your area is or you decide to adjust according to the Medicare rates. If you do use Medicare rates as your base, I recommend setting your out-of-pocket rates at one and a half to two times what Medicare pays.

If you're using psychotherapy codes, there are four that you'll likely use most often. They are:

90791—Initial Evaluation (Table 6.1)
90832—30-minute appointment
90834—45-minute appointment (Table 6.2)
90837—60-minute appointment

Until the procedure codes changed in 2013, the one most therapists used was for a 45-minute visit. Since that was the code I was used to, I take that out-of-pocket rate and add a certain amount for an initial evaluation, slightly less than the evaluation but more than the 90834 for my 60-minute visit, and then slightly less than the 90834 for the 30-minute visit. It's nice that we have the option for the 60-minute visits now because sometimes sessions do run long, and I appreciate being able to get paid for the extra time I spend with my patients.

Are you confused yet? Let's back up a step. Say your out-of-pocket rate is $100 for a standard 45-minutes session. You may then charge $125 for the initial evaluation, $115 for the hour-long visit, and $90 for a 30-minute visit. These are not recommended amounts, by the way. I'm keeping the numbers round to make the math easy.

How long are visits, actually? The following are the appropriate ranges (American Psychological Association, 2013):

90832—16 to 37 minutes
90834—38 to 52 minutes
90837—53 minutes or longer

For those of you who do family or couples' therapy, you have additional codes. I strongly suggest you consult with your professional organizations as to what those are and what changes occurred with the CPT codes starting in 2017. For example, there is a subtle change to the psychotherapy codes in that they no longer have "and/or family member" anymore. These codes are only for time spent with the patient.

We'll talk about documentation in Chapter 8, but be aware that you need to indicate the starting and ending time of each session whether or not you're billing insurance. You may be wondering why you would bill a 90832 session since most people talk in terms of a "therapy hour." You can only bill for time you spend face-to-face with clients, so if they're late or the session is otherwise truncated, you need to charge for a shorter session. It's a good motivator to discuss tardiness and other therapy-interfering (or shortening) behaviors with your clients. Sometimes life happens, and there's nothing you can do about it. I recently had a client who got a call from an elderly family member's doctor at the beginning of session. He had to leave to take the family member to the emergency room. Of course, I understood.

No one practices in a vacuum, and overhead in some areas is going to be more than in others. For example, when I started my practice, I was in a premium area for a health psychologist—within walking distance of two hospitals and a plethora of physicians' offices. I don't know that I could have afforded to be there had I not been in a space-sharing arrangement. When I moved closer to home in 2010, I came into the county seat, where I was now within walking distance of the courthouse. Space was still affordable until the city decided to embrace a "more density is better" approach. As residential property increased in value, so did commercial property. I could have raised my rates to compensate for it, but instead I moved. Another therapist I know did, however, raise her fees. I didn't blame her—she had bought into the property where she practiced, so she had literally invested in staying where she was.

Here are some factors to consider when you're setting your rates:

Overhead

One way to think of this might be that people generally expect to pay more for a higher level of service. Providing a higher level of service involves more overhead. For example, having office staff can add several hundred dollars a month or more to the budget, but clients appreciate being able to call and talk to a live human rather than leaving a message and playing phone tag with the provider, especially if they're calling for something like last-minute directions.

Having an office in a nicer building also costs more, as does providing coffee / tea service or water in the waiting room. In my previous office, rent was about to go up three dollars per square foot on the floor I was on because of the "premium view." All of this adds up.

It took me a while to recognize this in a real way, but what you pay yourself also falls under overhead and needs to be accounted for.

Area Characteristics and Demographics

Yes, this is tied to overhead but requires more detailed thinking about it. You'll likely see this reflected in your rent, which is part of overhead, but it's also important to consider the area you're working in. Are you setting up your office in an urban area, a suburb, or in a rural area? Services in general differ in price depending on where you are. It's okay to charge a higher price in the city than you would in the 'burbs. You might be tempted to charge lower than the competition, but then you run up against perceived value. No one wants to be known as the bargain therapist.

Experience

I was on a list-serv for a while where people put out calls for certain kinds of therapists for clients who needed extra help or who the therapists wanted to refer along. Often they'd specify, "experienced therapist only." I was never quite clear what made someone earn the title of "experienced," but I could see why that would matter. I definitely feel I'm a much better therapist now than I was ten or even five years ago. In the regular job world, experience is rewarded by raises and promotions. So, if you've been licensed and doing clinical work for several years, you have every right to charge more than someone who is just out of school or post-doc. Consider adding $10 or $20 an hour to what you determine the market rate to be.

Educational Level and Specialty

I put these two together because sometimes having a more advanced degree doesn't translate into better marketability. However, having a specialty area does, and from what I've seen, the more highly specialized someone is, the more they can charge, especially if it's a high-demand specialty. It comes down to basic economics—if a service is greatly needed, but there are only a few providers, the law of supply and demand dictates that the services will be more expensive. So, if you're the only therapist in the area who has several years of experience in a certain disorder with a certain population, focus on that in your marketing and feel free to charge a little more.

At this point, some of you may be squirming. *If you're in such a high-demand specialty,* you may be thinking, *shouldn't you charge less to make your services more accessible?*

There are several problems with this line of thinking. First, you're not acknowledging that you provide a valuable service, and you deserve to be compensated accordingly. Do you balk at spending more for a good massage therapist or hair stylist? If there was just one medical specialist that treated the specific problem you're suffering from, wouldn't you make the sacrifice to consult with them even if they weren't in your insurance network?

Second, whether or not you have student loans, you're still recouping on the investment you made in your training. Remember all those hours you spent learning your skills, the specialized trainings you paid for, and the effort you put forth in order to become not just knowledgeable but competent? They were an investment of both time and money, and this is your opportunity to collect a return on it. Don't forget, at this point your time has a price.

Third, I can speak from experience that while it's nice to be in a high-demand specialty, it can also be very stressful if not managed right. It's as stressful to have too many patients as to not have enough, and you run into the ethical dilemma of wanting to schedule as many people as possible but not having adequate opportunity for follow-up. If I were a neuropsychologist and my model was to see someone once or twice, it wouldn't be so bad, but most of those who do regular psychotherapy need to be able to see people weekly or at least biweekly. Limiting the number of patients one sees can be beneficial not only financially but ethically to ensure you can maintain the quality of care you're giving. I did stop taking new patients for a couple of months after a colleague left my practice and I inherited her caseload. I wouldn't recommend it because it frustrates referral sources and may lead them to start sending that particular type of patient to someone else, and it's difficult to tell when it's time to open up again. I wouldn't recommend stopping seeing new patients for more than two months, especially if your specialty is a time-limited technique with a finite number of visits in the protocol.

If you're not entirely comfortable with setting rates yet, here's another approach from the Smart Private Practice blog. They have a specific formula they suggest. First, figure out the market rate for your area. They suggest adding $10/hour for five years in practice and $20/hour for ten years. Then look at your finances and see what you need to bring in to make your overhead and pay yourself, but make sure "it feels authentic and valuable to you." Figure out what that minimum hourly rate would be, and then once you've built your caseload to the point you're bringing that in with the minimum number of clients required to make your overhead, slide it down for additional clients depending on need. I like the question they suggest posing to prospective clients: "I understand you would like a lower fee. My fees are currently $__. In your financial picture, is that possible?" (Smart Private Practice Blog, 2016). That way both the therapist and client have to ponder their own financial situations, and it allows the therapist to take a reduced rate or pro bono case. How far to slide can depend on insurance contracts, which I'll discuss later in this chapter.

One question I get frequently is whether it's permissible to charge clients different rates for the same service. I recommend that you have a standard out-of-pocket rate and slide or reduce as exceptions based on need. At this point, I don't reduce my rates except for very rarely. It can be tough to find that balance of charging higher rates that may frighten patients away but recoup income with making services accessible but then risking losing the perception of service quality.

Another way to open up accessibility is to take on trainees, who see patients on a sliding scale basis. I've had one practicum student in the past and currently have a post-doctoral fellow. I'll talk about trainees more in a future chapter. As with everything, there are advantages and disadvantages.

Software and Hardware

If you're not outsourcing your bookkeeping, you need a system for tracking expenses and income. My accountant recommended QuickBooks, a software package from Intuit, which helps to keep everything including banking information in one place. In this section, I'll talk about recommendations and how I use it.

One of your very first company assets will probably be your computer. The first thing you'll do with QuickBooks or whatever other accounting software you use is set up a company file. If you've installed it for the first time, it will ask you to set up your company the first time you open it. Your accountant can help you with this as well. I'm reluctant to give too many specific directions since you may be using a different product, and even if you do have

QuickBooks, the procedure may change slightly with each update, and I don't know how the Mac version may differ.

Once you've got your company set up, look at the left column. I always click on "View Balances" when I open it so I can keep track of how much is in my business checking and savings accounts and what my business credit card balance is. If you haven't gotten a business credit card yet, now is a good time. You can go ahead and set up your business checking and savings accounts here so you can keep track of expenses and transfers.

Your accounting software can be a powerful tool for both tracking where you spend money and how money comes in. A straightforward way to start tracking patient / client income is to first set up your item list. This is found in the lists menu in QuickBooks. Once you've got the item list pulled up, you'll add a new one by going to the item drop-down menu and choosing New Item, which will pop up another menu. I have mine set up with the code, the description under the description column, classified as a service, and categorized as fee for service income. So, for example, my 90791 might look like:

Table 6.1 Example Layout of a Service in Accounting Software

Name	Description	Type	Account	Rate
90791	Initial Evaluation	Service	Fee-for-service Income	$200

Note that the rate is for example purposes only, not a recommendation.

All of these categories match up with choices in the pop-up menu for each new item.

How do you set up clients so that each has their own account? First, think about how you want to label them. Remember, this file is going to your accountant, so if you're going to put in their names, you need to make sure you've got a business associate agreement and due diligence from them. These are good ideas, anyway. Before I learned about compliance, I was concerned about confidentiality in my accountant's file, so I started assigning each client a chart number that ends up being the name for their QuickBooks file. I stole my numbering system from my previous employer, which is to start with the year digits and then the order the patient came into the practice as a new patient. So, my first patient of 2017 was given the chart number 17001, the second one 17002, and so on. A bonus for this system is that it's easy to see approximately how long patients have been coming just by looking at their chart numbers. Before I record charges or payments, I'll match up the chart number with the patient so I can make sure everything is categorized correctly.

There are two ways to set up a client account. I usually do this at the first visit so chart numbers are only assigned to people who come in. The easiest way is to click on the Statements icon in the company home screen (green ledger box in the P.C. version), and when it pops up, click on the Customer:Job drop-down, and choose <Add New>. Put the chart number in the Customer Name box and click OK. You're all set up.

The more complicated way is to go to the Customers menu and choose Customers Center. Click on New Customer and Job and choose New Customer. That will bring up the same box.

If you're using a different software from QuickBooks, ask your account-ant to take some time helping you set things up. You can bring this chapter with you so he or she will know what you need. I run my business off my laptop, which has some security risks, but at least I can bring it with me to my accountant's office if needed. That's actually what I did when I interviewed Kelly Locklear of Small Business Solutions for this chapter as there were some things I didn't know how to do, even eight years into using QuickBooks for my practice. Whatever software you choose, make sure it's flexible enough to handle business expansion and adding different services. For example, I've had to figure out how to enter book royalties and speaking honoraria so they show up correctly in my reports.

The Insurance Conundrum

In a conversation with one of my business-coaching clients, I described my opinion on dealing with insurance companies as follows: it's like having a prolonged conversation with someone who has a severe personality disorder, where their reality only barely overlaps yours. Ninety percent of the time, dealing with insurance companies is fine, but that last ten percent can be frus-trating. This is something I have to explain to the new providers who join my practice—no, sometimes it's not going to make sense. One recent exam-ple is that one of the insurance companies I'm in-network for went ahead and changed their diagnosis codes according to the DSM-5 almost as soon as the new DSM came out. However, some of the DSM codes were in error. A supplement with the correct ones was later published before the national code change deadline, but that particular insurance company never corrected it in their system. Consequently, whenever I see a patient with that insurance, I have to enter the diagnosis code that was in the original, uncorrected DSM. Patients have suggested to me that it would be an easy fix in their system. Perhaps it would, perhaps it wouldn't, but it's one of those things that just doesn't make sense but that I have to adjust for.

The major disadvantage of taking insurance from a provider's perspective is that the hourly rate ends up being much lower than if you were accepting self-pay patients only. A second, slightly less major disadvantage is that if insurance companies are paying you, they sometimes try to control certain aspects of your business in the name of cost saving. While I haven't seen them limit the number of sessions like they used to before mental health parity passed, they have other ways of trying to manage how you treat your patients. For example, I have noticed one payer in particular sending letters every quarter with the number of 30-minute, 45-minute, and 60-minute sessions I've billed and comparing them to "other providers in the area." If I go above a certain percentage of the longer visits, there's a threat of record audit. So, rather than leaving it up to me as the provider to determine how long I spend with my clients, I could potentially be penalized for charging too many long sessions.

Filing insurance for mental health visits has some disadvantages for clients, too. The biggest is that we do have to assign diagnoses and then file them. These can later be pulled up by life and other health insurance companies, which can result in future coverage being denied. With this in mind, some patients have declined to use their insurance coverage and instead paid me in cash to make sure the only records of their visits would be mine. Another disadvantage, according to Bill Herring, LCSW, who has a fantastic explanation on his website as to why he does not take insurance, is that claims pass through many sets of hands—or now, across many computer screens—before payment is issued. Although these employees are held to high standards of confidentiality, it's still a risk to the patients' information. This is the case whether you're in-network or out-of-network since you're sending information to the insurance company either way (B. Herring, personal communication, January 23, 2017).

So what is a provider to do? When you're starting out, you definitely want to build up a referral stream as soon as possible, and getting on insurance panels can be very helpful for this. On the other hand, you don't want to hamstring yourself down the road by having your schedule crowded with clients for whom you're not being paid enough per visit to meet your overhead and pay yourself. Some providers are established enough in their community from previous employment or through effective marketing to start off not taking any insurance. They may build more slowly, but they are receiving more money per hour, so two hours of their face-to-face time with client hours brings in what three would for a provider who would see those patients and be paid by their insurance.

The traditional way to approach insurance is to work on getting on as many insurance panels as possible and then slowly drop off once you've become established and need to start limiting patient flow. One of the therapists I interviewed called this the "therapist's trap," and more than one of my interviewees said they wished they'd known they didn't have to be on insurance panels to be successful. In my experience, insurance credentialing ends up being a lot of work on the front end, and it can be difficult for both the provider and the clients on the back end when you decide to stop taking their insurance, especially for long-term clients. Of course, you want to then make ethical referrals so they can continue getting care somewhere else if they decide not to continue with you.

While researching this book, I came across an interesting hybrid approach. Julie Kolzet, PhD, who practices in Manhattan, told me she researched who the biggest payer in her area was and then got paneled only for that payer. That way she had a referral stream of patients starting out, especially since she was already known to a lot of the physicians in the area, but she also had plenty of room on her schedule for self-pay clients (J. Kolzet, personal communication, November 9, 2016). I've come to the same result the opposite way in that I started off taking five types of insurance, and as of the end of 2016, was down to two. I based which ones I kept on my professional affiliation with a nearby large university and associated agencies.

Should you decide to proceed with becoming paneled, the first step is to register with CAQH, the Council for Affordable Quality Healthcare (http://www.caqh.org/solutions/caqh-proview/). It's essentially a database where you go in and put in your information so that insurance companies can theoretically access it. This supposedly keeps you from having to give the same information to each different insurance company when you apply to be on their provider panel. Be forewarned—there is still a lot of redundant information you have to provide, and by the end of the process, you'll be able to rattle off your individual and group NPI's and your tax I.D. number by heart. You may even start doing so in your sleep. It depends on how many insurance contracts you're going for.

There are two ways to get a CAQH I.D. number. The first is to approach one of the insurance companies you want to be a provider for and ask them to issue one for you. Yes, in order to be on insurance panels, you need to have a CAQH number, but in order to get a CAQH number, you have to approach the insurance companies and request one through them, which can take weeks. See what I mean about logic, or lack thereof?

But never fear—if you want to spend the money, other options are available. You can pay certain services a fee for an "expedited application," and they'll get the I.D. number so you can go ahead and start filling out your application. My thought is that since you're already going to be agreeing to take discounted payments from insurance companies, you shouldn't have to lose even more money and pay on the front end, but I leave that up to you. Just make sure you go with a reputable service.

Once you get your CAQH I.D. number, you go in and fill out a very long form with many parts, and then you upload supporting documents. This has gotten much easier since they've gone to uploading rather than faxing. You'll still have to approach the provider credentialing departments of the insurance companies you want to be in-network for and ask them for applications. This is also not necessarily an easy task, and it can require a lot of time and patience. Once you give them the information they need, most of which you put on the CAQH form, and they approve your application, they'll send you contracts. Some of them have contracts for each of their plan types, and some have a general one. Many will go ahead and send you their Medicare private plan contracts as well.

When you receive the contracts, you'll see what their reimbursement rates are. Consider setting a lower limit for what you will accept per hour based on your financial situation and needs. Also beware of contracts that say they'll pay you a ridiculously low fee for a period of time, often a year, with the promise to negotiate it after that time expires. Often they won't, and then you've been stuck with a schedule crowded with patients you're being paid little for.

As with any contracts, it's a good idea to be cautious when dealing with ones from insurance companies. They'll typically have a clause stating that theirs cannot be the highest rate you accept, meaning you'll need to set your out-of-pocket/out-of-network fees higher. You can slide lower, but the bottom of your sliding scale cannot be lower than the lowest contracted insurance rate you accept. So, for example, if the lowest insurance rate I'm paid for a 90834 (45-minute) visit is $72, I can't have any sliding scale fees lower than $72.01. On the other end, if the highest insurance rate I have is $125, I cannot set my out-of-pocket fee for the same level of visit lower than $125.01. See how that works? By accepting insurance, you're limiting what you can do with your rates. Sometimes you can negotiate with insurance companies for higher rates, especially if you have a specialty with extra certification, but many large insurance companies won't. It never hurts to ask, though.

Sometimes insurance company contracts have strange clauses. For example, one I looked at had a clause that I had to submit all marketing materials to them for approval. When I asked about that clause, the company didn't clarify it but instead informed me that they were so big they couldn't negotiate different contracts for different providers. I didn't sign that one, which, by the way, was one of the private Medicare contracts.

Here are some terms to be familiar with:

Contracted Rate

This is the rate you agree to accept for seeing a patient who has insurance you're in-network for. This differs by type of insurance and level of insurance, but clients within those levels will have the same rates. For example, if one client has Cheapo Insurance PPO, the contracted rate may be different for a client who has Cheapo Insurance HMO, but all clients who have Cheapo PPO plans will have the same rates as each other.

Copay

A fixed amount a client has to pay for each visit.

Coinsurance

A percentage of the visit cost a client has to pay. Many insurance plans will require one or the other. Some require both. Yes, the math can get confusing. Let's say you have a contracted rate of $100 for a visit for a certain patient, who will owe a $10 copay and 10 percent coinsurance. The patient cost will be $19 if the insurance company calculates the coinsurance based on the session rate after the copay is subtracted. However, if the coinsurance is taken first, it will be $20. Thankfully this situation is rare.

Credentialing

The process for becoming a network provider for an insurance company. Often you will approach their credentialing department to start the process.

Deductible

The amount a patient has to pay themselves before insurance will start paying you for seeing them. This differs between individual plans. Recently, high deductible plans have become in-vogue, so people end up paying out of pocket for a lot. There are two different types of deductibles:

1. Family deductible: the amount of money members of a family have to pay before insurance benefits kick in for the family members. The good news is that if one member of the family requires a lot of health services

and meets the family deductible (and their individual one on the way), the benefits activate for the entire family.

2. Individual deductible: the amount of money one family member has to pay before insurance benefits kick in. These are all applied to the family deductible.

In-Network

This means a provider has a contract with the insurance company. Benefits for the provider include more referrals because a lot of people want to use their insurance benefits, which will allow them to pay less for services and they often end up being listed on the insurance website, where people can search for providers by specialty and location. Insurance companies promise to limit the number of providers on their panel. Benefits to the insurance companies include paying providers less for services.

Out-of-Network

A provider is out of network when they do not have a contract with an insurance company.

Out-of-Pocket Maximum

The amount a client pays total across a year before the insurance company has to pay for the entire cost of services. Typically, patients who meet their OOP maximums have had a major health event, for example, a surgery or psychiatric hospitalization. Once they hit that number, they won't have to pay copays or coinsurances until the next insurance year. Note I said insurance year, not calendar year. Many insurance plans will start everything over—including deductibles—on January 1. However, not all of them do. For example, if the plan is associated with an academic institution, it may reset everything according to the academic year.

Panel

This is a group of providers who are in-network for a specific insurance company.

After you see a patient and file the visit, you'll receive an Explanation of Benefits (EOB), as will the patients. Often the clients receive them before the providers. The EOB's will show the visit code, amount the provider charged, and if you're in-network for the insurance company, you'll see the discount they took (difference between what you charged and the contracted rate), copay and/or coinsurance, and what they'll pay you as well as any codes. The key to the codes is on the back or bottom of the EOB, so if they denied the charge, you can see why.

When you take insurance, setting up your accounting software item list gets a little more complicated. When you file insurance, you'll always submit the full cost of the session code (e.g., $150 for a 90834 if $150 is your out-of-pocket rate for a 45-minute psychotherapy session), but for your own finances, you'll want to know what each patient owes based on the contract rate for that particular insurance company. I have mine set up that each item has sub-items, one for each insurance contract. So, it looks something like this:

Table 6.2 Example of How to Set Up Different Insurance Rates in Accounting Software

Item	Subitem	Rate
90834		$120
	90834 – Insurance A	$86
	90834 – Insurance B	$95
	90834 – Insurance C	$75

Note that the rate is for example purposes only, not a recommendation.

I've made these numbers up, by the way, and kept them round for the sake of the example. When you set up these items in QuickBooks, you click on the Subitem of box and choose the item you're putting it under. They'll still be classified as fee-for-service income.

If I have a self-pay patient, I just click on 90834 for that day's visit. If I have a patient who has Insurance B, I click on 90834—Insurance B for that visit. This is helpful because let's say it's the beginning of the year, and the patient, who has Insurance B, has to meet a deductible, but somehow you don't know this until after you've filed the visit. Remember, with a deductible, the in-network insurance client has to pay the entire negotiated rate for each visit until the deductible is met. That patient's account is showing that they were charged $20 for their copay. You want to know that the balance is then $75, which is the contracted rate of $95 minus the $20 they've paid.

Yes, this is confusing. My office manager and I still have to have conversations when our math differs during deductible season.

As if deductibles weren't confusing enough, the insurance companies can decide to apply the in-network rate to the deductible even if you're not on their panel. So let's say the patient above has Insurance D, who you're not in-network for, and their contracted rate for a 90834 is only $70. Even though the patient ends up paying $120 total for the session, their insurance company may only apply $70 toward the deductible. It's important to be able to explain to the patients that we have no control over what the insurance company applies to the deductible, and no, we don't owe them $50 in this situation. It's one way insurance companies encourage their subscribers to stick with in-network providers.

I've already discussed the discounted rates they make in-network providers take and how they'll often only apply that to a patient's deductible when they see out-of-network providers. One other trick they'll pull is to send you a letter, usually via fax, promising to pay you sooner if you agree to take a reduced rate. Don't ever agree to this—they still have to pay you in a timely manner even if you don't agree. I have my office manager write in bold across the bottom of the letter, 'PROVIDER DOES NOT NEGOTIATE' and fax it back to them. Sometimes they'll persist, even to the point on insisting on a phone call, and you'll have to talk to them, but hold your ground. You're not 'delaying' payment if you don't agree to their reduced terms, you're getting paid the full amount you can get, or the most possible is applied to the patient's deductible. I've tried to tell the intermediary service who makes these calls on behalf of the insurance companies to not even try to contact me about reduced rates, but they of course refuse to put a general rule in the system and contact me for every single visit for every single case.

Medicare: Insurance Meets Government Bureaucracy

One major insurance decision faced by most providers is whether to take Medicare. Please don't misunderstand me—when I've had to call Medicare, the people who work there are very nice, but it's still a large government agency with the associated bureaucracy. I can't speak to Medicaid since in my state, it doesn't recognize psychotherapy as a valid treatment for adults over age 18, but I'm guessing dealing with it is similarly complicated.

The process of getting on Medicare should've been my first clue as to what the experience would be like. I had to submit my application four times. I had it right the first time. By the way, when you submit your application, you have to go through your regional office, not the central Medicare office.

Once you get paneled with Medicare, there's extra paperwork. First, you have to recertify every five years or so, which means you essentially have to go through the entire application process again. Even better—you have to do it for both your individual NPI and your group NPI. The last time I did it, something wasn't connecting in the computer system, so I had to send in a paper application. Which they then lost.

Pro tip—any time you send something in to an insurance company, make sure you send it certified mail with a return receipt. This saved me this last time. I was able to call and say who signed for the application, and they tracked it down and put it through.

The other extra fun of Medicare is PQRS, Physician Quality Reporting System, requirements. This means that for a certain percentage of visits—over 50 percent for most of the measures—you have to report on different aspects of the patients' health *whether they're relevant to what you're doing with the patients or not*. If you don't, you get penalized a small percentage of each visit, which adds up. It was possible for mental health practitioners in small practices like mine to meet at least minimum reporting requirements—even though they annoyed the patients, who didn't understand why I wasted time asking them about certain non-relevant things each visit—until a couple of years ago. I didn't even try to report for 2015 because I knew I wouldn't meet the minimums. Plus, entering all the parameters for all the visits takes time and requires you to spend at least $200 on a reporting service. While these reporting requirements are supposed to enhance patient care, they don't fulfill that goal.

What about the private Medicare plans? They don't require reporting, but they have their own issues. For example, one of the major ones decided in the middle of 2016 to stop paying for psychotherapy for insomnia, which is most of what I do. Those patients were stuck owing for their visits, and I lost a lot of money. Since I'm conservative with diagnoses, and I prefer to not commit insurance fraud, I couldn't just stick an adjustment disorder on them and refile if it didn't fit.

Another frustration of Medicare is that it only pays 80 percent of visits, and patients have to pay the rest unless they have a secondary insurance that will supposedly cover it. So you're stuck with two insurances, not one, and sometimes the secondary won't pay for whatever reason. We still have to charge the coinsurance and document that we pursued payment because not to do so would be insurance fraud.

If you do take Medicare, make sure you keep some money in reserve at the end of the year. Why? Medicare, like many insurance companies, has a deductible that it requires at the beginning of the year, typically around $160. The secondary insurance will pay it for most patients, but you won't see that money until February at the earliest since Medicare takes two to three weeks to send the EOB with the amount showed applied to the deductible, and then the claim gets sent to the secondary insurance company, either manually or automatically. Then the secondary insurance takes another two to three weeks to pay.

I have other examples of why Medicare has not been the easiest insurance to deal with, but I won't bore you with them. I sent in my opt-out letter to be off Medicare at the end of 2016. I hate losing some of those patients, but it just got to the point where it wasn't worth the extra time and effort, particularly in light of the PQRS penalties.

At this point, certain practices are exempt from reporting requirements, so if you really want to take Medicare, check and see if yours may be one of them.

Please understand, I'm not saying you shouldn't take Medicare. If you're a geropsychologist, it may match up with your practice goals. Whether or not to accept Medicare is one area where it's important to look at your practice values and consider balance.

Budget

Setting a budget for your business is similar to setting one for your home, except with your practice you get to pay yourself. You also don't get to buy wine, or you shouldn't, but that's okay.

The first thing to consider is what you'll have to pay for each month. Rent is an obvious one, as are utilities (if applicable), cleaning (if you have to arrange for it yourself), telephone, and internet service. These will go into your budget spreadsheet first, and they probably won't change very much, so you can fill them in for the year if you like. I counted parking as a rent expense in my QuickBooks file but accounted for it on a separate line in my budget since the number of patient parking vouchers I needed fluctuated from month to month.

Other monthly costs that won't fluctuate much include software subscriptions and fees. Software companies like Microsoft and Intuit have been moving to a subscription-based model, where, instead of paying a lot of money once for a license to use the software, you end up paying a certain fee monthly for it. For example, I have a Microsoft 365 subscription, which allows me to have Word, PowerPoint, and Excel running on my computer. Rather than having a Microsoft Office license, I have a subscription and pay a fee each month. The nice thing is that they'll automatically update to the newest version, which has to happen occasionally anyway. It's also easy to reinstall software if I have problems. I do have a traditional QuickBooks license, though. So far I've balked at doing the online QuickBooks thing because I don't want to be without access to my financial records if my internet company is having a bad day. I also have an internet fax service since a lot of the medical world is still kind of stuck in the 1990s in some respects.

When I set up my budget spreadsheet, I put payroll in a different place, although it all gets added in the end. It helps me mentally to keep it separate, but you're welcome to put it in with your regular monthly expenses. You can see what I mean with my example spreadsheet. I also put my payroll taxes there.

Other areas on the budget may start low and increase as you begin to make more money. For example, if you take credit cards, those fees are based on percentage of sales. Your fees will start low, grow, and top out once you have a full caseload. If you're in an office building where you can validate parking, you won't need as many at first. Office supplies and what I deem environmental comforts (still coded as office expenses) like water service and coffee or tea are also items that will require a smaller budget at first and larger one later. While you'll need basic office supplies at first, you can add the environmental comforts in gradually unless you really want them at first. Postage is one area that may go the opposite, in that you'll spend more on stamps at first as you get your marketing going.

When you're first setting up an office, you'll need to budget for items like furniture and equipment. If your filing cabinets and copier stand are going to be out of patient sight, you can get good prices on less attractive or used pieces. However, that's what I did, and then we moved into an office where there isn't a closet, so now the world gets to see my cool, funky dark purple filing cabinet. I don't care what anyone says—I like my purple filing cabinet, and it looks lovely on the blue carpet. This is another area where you can start with the basics and add more later. At the very least you'll need a computer, scanner, and printer. Having one that will print two-sided is much more useful, but don't waste the money on splurging for a color printer.

Other one-time costs may include legal advice on leases or incorporation. An unexpected cost I've had twice now is having to pay someone to run Ethernet cable at the office after I've moved in. Even if the wires are there, you may still need to have someone come out and hook everything up—alas, your internet company won't do everything for you—so set a few hundred dollars aside for that.

Now that you've got your startup and monthly costs figured out, let's think annually. As the name implies, these are costs that you'll only pay once a year. You'll need to pay your accountant at tax time. You also need malpractice, general liability, and maybe workman's comp insurances, which can often be paid in installments, but beware of installment fees. I was paying my GLI/ WC insurance monthly for a while, but I went to quarterly when I figured out each statement came with a $6 fee. Actually, check anything that allows you to pay in increments for a statement or installment fee—there's no reason to spend money you don't need to.

You're a licensed professional, which means you'll likely need to accrue continuing education hours. What about those costs? These will vary by distance traveled. We're fortunate here in the Atlanta area to have many opportunities for continuing education. When I stay local, I typically only have to pay the registration fee and possibly for a meal out. There's something to be said for going to conferences, though, especially when you're in a niche field and don't have many fellow practitioners in your area. I typically go to two conferences per year, so I have to budget in conference registration, travel expenses, and meals. Plus, membership fees since I'm a member of the organizations who hosts those conferences. I like to budget for my conferences separately so I can keep money aside or shift it around more easily if needed. Other annual costs may include website hosting and domain registration. Somehow, I always forget those in my budget, so they get lumped in with computer and internet costs, which is not the most accurate way to look at them. If you use Amazon Prime to order things for your business, you can count that registration as well. You also have to have money for those reference books and the new treatment manual for that therapeutic thing that you do.

You can't think about budget without pondering how the government wants to take their share. You'll need to renew your business license annually with the city or county you're in, and the Secretary of State's office will want their annual corporation renewal fee. In Georgia, we renew our state psychology licenses biannually. Then there are county, state, and city property taxes.

One area you may have noticed I haven't said anything about is marketing. Costs for this will vary as you hit different stages in your career. The most important lesson I've learned—and this has been echoed by most of the psychologists I interviewed for this book—is that the best way to market is to build relationships with referral sources, or the people who will send clients your way. Just as with the rest of the budget, you can think about your marketing budget in tiers. The first is the setup tier. Unless you're a graphic design wizard, you will likely need to pay someone to come up with a logo and website design for you, and you may need to hire a content designer. I'll talk more about the website in the marketing chapter, but you will need a line in your budget for domain registration and hosting. Then you'll need the basics like business cards. I've recently come to appreciate brochures, too, because they're a great leave-behind and give people an idea of your practice without having to visit your website. You know, in case their internet provider or your website hosting service is having a bad day.

Finally, it's always a good idea to have some cash on hand for unexpected expenses, sort of an emergency fund. You also want to set aside some of your profits to reinvest in your business. I try to set aside money in my savings account each month for these purposes.

One thing to be very careful about is to not use business funds for personal expenses and vice versa. This is the number one business owner mistake seen by Carly Berg of Above & Beyond Bookkeeping, which is based in Atlanta, although she's worked in Miami and New York as well. The second mistake is not putting enough money away for taxes. As for how much, she recommends talking to your accountant to advise you. She also cautions business owners to be careful about what they try to expense (C. Berg, personal communication, January 13, 2017).

At this point, you may be feeling overwhelmed. It's a lot to think about, but doing so now will help you be prepared later. The good news is that you have control over the amount you put in a lot of these categories, and it's fine to start small. Some categories may overlap. For example, going to continuing education workshops is a great way to meet other providers and network, so it gives you the opportunity to market yourself.

The Business of Business

I will admit that for a long time, I only paid attention to what the practice brought in and what I spent without making any effort to understand basic business principles. One of my patients, himself an entrepreneur, gave me a stack of his old business books, and they opened my eyes to see my business in a new way. I recommend picking up and reading some of these resources for yourself. I'll do my best to summarize the very basic principles, but I don't have business training beyond my attempts at self-study. I don't think you need to have an MBA in order to have a successful business, but it does help to develop what's called business acumen, or an idea of how all the moving parts move together. This is a step that many small business owners skip, but it's necessary. An advantage of a small business like a private practice is that you're able to make changes quickly, but first you need to know that you need to make them.

This is embarrassing, and my friends who have a business background will be facepalming at this, but here's my big real-life mistake. I've had the tendency of only watching the money that came in, which is actually thought of as the "top line" of the business statement, and the balances in my business checking and savings accounts. As long as I made enough money to meet my monthly income goals and had positive numbers in my accounts, I thought I was fine. One year in September, I ran a Profit & Loss Statement, often referred to as "the P&L," which needs to be a cocktail name, to see where things were in anticipation of an office move. I had money in my checking and savings accounts, and I continued to bring in income, but the bottom line of the report, which showed the profit, was down drastically from the previous year.

So what happened? In a broad sense, the bottom line is calculated by subtracting expenses from income. I lost a contract psychologist at the beginning of the year, so my income was down, although not drastically. She hadn't reached the point of building her practice where her caseload had increased dramatically—that would have happened had she stayed even another month. I'd inherited her patients and managed a healthy referral stream, so I was super busy through the spring and summer.

Since income was fine—not great, but fine—the major hit to my bottom line came from my expenses. Specifically, I had been putting as much money into a side venture, which is tied to the practice, as the previous year, but I hadn't been bringing as much in. Other expenses that hadn't occurred the previous year included increased education costs, mostly online workshops, both for my fiction books and in anticipation of this book coming out. There were also anticipatory costs of moving such as pre-paying first month's rent and security deposit. I also traveled a lot for both careers. Although I'd budgeted for the travel, the expenses had occurred mostly in the first three quarters.

How did I adjust to correct my mistake? The last quarter is a particularly tough one because of time off and lighter schedule around the holidays. I cut the amount I paid myself and my shareholder payments so I could ensure I'd have enough cash on hand for the move and operating expenses with the consideration that income would be down. If I hadn't adjusted, I would have ended up with insufficient funds and may have had to shift over personal assets.

Here is how to avoid making the same mistake I did and keep an eye on the financial health of your practice.

First, read some business books or take an online course to learn the applicable terms and how it all should theoretically work. I'm going to give you an overview, but I really encourage you to do some studying on your own. I've listed some books I've found helpful in the References.

Second, learn the terms. Here are some that you need to know, which you'll see on your income statement:

Income Statement

I figured that's a good place to start. This is where you see how the business did over a specific time frame. For example, you can run an income statement for a day, week, month, quarter, year... Whatever you define. It's also referred to as the Profit and Loss Statement, P&L, Statement of Operations, and Statement of Earnings (Cope, 2012).

To find your Income Statement in QuickBooks, go to Reports -> Company & Financial -> Profit & Loss Standard or Profit & Loss Detail. The standard view will give you the total under each category heading, whereas the detail view shows you every transaction. I find it more useful to look at the cash view, which brings us to:

Cash Basis vs. Accrual Basis

Business accountants typically look at the accrual view, which is the income that was billed during a certain period (Sobel, 2010). I prefer the cash view, which is the money that actually came in. One of the unfortunate realities of private practice is that sometimes we don't get paid, so I like to see the money I have rather than the money I should have. The default in QuickBooks is the accrual view, so to change it, in the report view, go to Customize Report (button on the top left in my version), and then in the second block down, click the radio button for Cash and then the big blue OK button.

Expense

This is the money you spend, pretty much everything in your budget. In the standard view, you get only the total for each category, and in the detail view, you can see each transaction.

Net Income

Also known as profit, this is calculated by subtracting expenses from cash. This is the best measure of your company's financial health.

Now that you know what the terms mean, consider doing the following:

For the first year, run a P&L statement at the end of each month and at the end of the quarter. The monthly ones should be in detail view so you can see where your money is going. For example, when I looked back at the first year of my practice, I saw great fluctuation in the expense number and traced it to conference registration and travel (worth it) and purchased ads (so not worth it). The quarterly ones will give you the information you need in standard view, which is income, expenses, and profit. Hopefully, you'll see that if you are taking a loss at the beginning, it's getting smaller with each successive month and quarter, and expenses may fluctuate with startup and travel costs but should even out to a certain range. Looking at these things monthly can help you see where expenses need to be reined in. Once you're established, you can look at biannual trends to check on the overall health of the business (G. Parnaby, personal communication, January 30, 2017).

As Kevin Cope (2012) states in *Seeing the Big Picture*, his excellent book on business acumen, companies can increase the bottom line by either increasing income or decreasing expenses. Monitoring your financial statements can help you see where you can do each and how it all balances out.

Conclusion

As with many aspects of doing therapy, getting the financial aspects of your business exactly right takes time and has a certain art to it. I'd like to take the opportunity to reiterate my point from Chapter 4—this is an excellent place to seek help and delegate, particularly when it comes to accounting. A good accountant will help you to set up your accounting software and give you an idea of how to code your expenses. They can also answer questions about what you can write off. Even so, you can't not pay attention. As I found, you can't be too careful when it comes to monitoring the bottom line.

One area where you have to spend money to make money is marketing, which I'll discuss in the next chapter.

Box 6.1 Interview with the Expert: Kelly Locklear

I wanted to make sure I gave you the best information possible about accounting and other financial matters, so I scheduled a meeting with Kelly Locklear of Small Business Solutions to go over my file and make sure I'm doing everything right. It also gave me the opportunity to ask her some questions. You've probably already noticed some of Kelly's wisdom in Chapter 4.

Our interview was recorded, so rather than following the usual Interview with the Expert box, I'll summarize.

The first question I asked Kelly was what the biggest benefit of a business using QuickBooks or another accounting software is. For her, it came down to three words: correct financial statements. "We can't prepare an accurate tax return necessarily without correct financials," she told me. "You can't go to the bank and get the loan, you can't do a refile, you can't really do any kind of professional financial transactions without financial statements." She noted that she's done Profit & Loss statements on spreadsheets, but that's a lot of work, and banks won't accept them, anyway. Also, in an audit situation, those financial statements are often what the IRS will ask for after the bank statements.

My next question was about what she says to people who don't feel they have the time to learn one more thing, one more piece of software. She identified keeping up with the books as one of the basic responsibilities of a business owner. She added, "There are a fair number of people that think they just don't have the capacity for that. They'll make the excuse that they don't have the time, but what it's really about is that they're afraid of the numbers and don't want to deal with it because they're afraid of getting it wrong. You do it anyway and then call your accountant and get all the kinks sorted out."

I thought this was a really good point. Just as we're ethically and legally responsible for providing the best care we can to our patients, we have a similar level of responsibility for our businesses. She also pointed out that having the correct information can help her and other accountants find deductions at tax time.

I had been concerned I was missing something, so my next question was about mistakes people tend to make. Just as it's important for us to make accurate diagnoses, coding financial transactions correctly is key. The biggest coding error she sees is when businesspeople code purchases incorrectly, particularly assets vs. expenses. She pointed out that copy paper is an expense because it's something we go through, but a computer should be classified as an asset. The definition of an asset according to her: "Something durable, something that will last more than a year, and typically costs more than $200." There is a QuickBooks category that is furniture/equipment, so that's where things like computers, cell phones, and furniture go. Other things are classified under "office expense" (K. Locklear, personal communication, December 9, 2016).

There are subtleties, however. I asked about the pictures I just got framed, each of which cost just over $200 to do, and which I hope to have for several years. She said to classify them as an office expense. I guess I'll just let my accountant sort that out.

Bibliography

American Psychological Association. (2013). More Q&As about the New Psychotherapy Codes [downloadable pdf]. *Good Practice, 2013* (Winter). Retrieved from http://www. apapracticecentral.org/good-practice/new-psychotherapy-codes.pdf.

Cope, K. (2012). *Seeing the big picture: Business acumen to build your credibility, career, and company.* Austin, Texas: Greenleaf Book Group Press.

Smart Private Practice Blog. (2016). Determine Your Practice Fees: Ready, Set...Collect [blog post]. Retrieved from https://blog.smartprivatepractice.com/2016/12/02/ determine-your-practice-fees-ready-set-collect/.

Sobel, M. (2010). *MBA in a nutshell.* New York, New York: McGraw-Hill.

Marketing Strategy   **7**

Typically the words "marketing" and "self-promotion" will give a therapist hives. We don't like promoting ourselves. It's uncomfortable. We'd rather be finding out about other people and helping them with their problems. Lack of clients can be a problem, but it's not one we enjoy fixing, although the result is nice. The good news is that we've already got the skills to be good at this, or at least not terrible. One colleague did decline to be interviewed for my book because they (gender-neutral pronoun for anonymity) didn't feel they were successful in practice, but they admitted they didn't want to put forth the effort to build the necessary relationships. They obviously had a great aversion to this very necessary activity.

It's okay to be nervous about marketing, but you have to get over yourself. Your anxiety is not more important than building your practice. If it was, you wouldn't have started on this path. I hope in this chapter to de-mystify and strip the terror from three words that tend to give us as psychologists hives: marketing, branding, and networking. I'll also give you a couple of cautionary tales, one about a mistake I made and one about a marketing mishap.

When it comes to marketing, it helps to know who you're marketing to. You may want to look at your business plan and at the population you identified in Chapter 5 and identify who your ideal client is. The worksheet at the end of Chapter 5 hopefully helped you to identify the parameters that will define your marketing strategy.

Once you determine who your ideal client is, the next step is to figure out where to find that person. What do they like to do? Where do they hang out? Where will they look for services like yours?

Or, even better, who can you approach to send your ideal clients to you?

While direct-to-consumer marketing has its place, your budget will be better spent targeting those who will funnel the clients to you, namely, referral sources.

If you learn nothing else from this chapter, remember this—marketing is all about the relationships.

Branding

Before you market your practice, you first need to figure out what your practice's brand is. If you're like me, the first thing you picture when you read the word "branding" is a painful experience. I'm talking about the discomfort of confining yourself into a little box, not the heat-branding kind of pain, although you may be motivated to avoid both equally. The thing is, branding isn't confining so much as it's about consistency.

Think about some famous brands. I'm in Atlanta, so one of the big ones that comes to mind is Coca Cola. I don't consume a lot of their products, but I'm likely to recognize one when I see it, at least the soft drinks. Think about what makes a Coke product recognizable. They use a certain color palette, bright but not jewel tones. They use certain fonts on their cans, and they have sort of curvy swoops and swooshes on them. And I bet most of you would recognize the shape of an empty glass Coke bottle even if you couldn't see the logo imprinted on it. Even if you'd never tasted one of their products, you may feel like you had an idea of what they'd be like from the accumulation of these shapes and images, and those expectations would be cemented by what you see on commercials.

So when people see you or materials from your practice, what do you want them to think of? Kim Garst of Boom! Social defines brand most succinctly when she calls it the impression of you and your product (Garst, December 2016). She works in the online world, but she has great resources for any business. The good news—you've probably already started thinking about your brand without realizing it.

One example of the general psychologist brand, and a not necessarily positive one, is the joke about psychologist fashion, or lack thereof. Have you ever heard comments about the therapist "look"? One of my grad school colleagues posted on Facebook that she'd been to a CEU event and had never seen so many clogs and printed turtlenecks in one place. I had to laugh and cringe. Granted, that was several years ago. To be clear, I have never owned any clogs or printed turtlenecks, and I certainly don't judge those who do, but I understood what she was talking about. We tend to dress conservatively, avoid bright colors, and go for comfortable shoes. Not that there's anything wrong with any of that. We likely choose our work wardrobes to convey a comforting, nonthreatening demeanor for our clients, and we want our clothing to be comfortable since we can have long days. One way to think about it is that I'm not going to wear a top hat and corset to see clients, but I'm also not going to wear the same outfit to my practice as I do to a science fiction and fantasy convention.

Your branding starts with you and the first impression you want to cultivate. I tend to dress business casual at the office to show I'm a competent professional and that I'm serious about what I do. My makeup tends to be minimalist—okay, that's partially because I'm not a morning person—and I have naturally curly hair, which has its unruly days thanks to our Georgia humidity. It fits me because I can be serious and reserved, but I use my creativity and humor in session. My office is decorated in neutral colors with a few fun but subtle touches such as my prints of Pete the Cat and a collection of toys and stuffed animals that I've collected, or patients have given me, on top of my bookcase. That area gives me some room to play and allow my geeky persona to come through. My science-fiction-minded patients usually hone in on the stuffed Dalek up there, and when they comment on it, it gives us a point of connection. The office is also quiet with cushions of white noise between rooms. Basically, I'm going for a peaceful atmosphere that, perhaps ironically, isn't so relaxing as to put people to sleep.

Now let's move outside the practice and the impression you want to bring to the world. If you look at the first element of your business plan, specifically why you're passionate about your business, think about how that can translate to your logo. Some psychologists don't have a logo, but without one, it's harder to put together marketing materials like cards and letterhead. For example, my graphic designer gave me files with different elements that match my logo colors and shape. She also designed my website, so it all has a consistent look and feel. Most importantly, all of it evokes my passion for bringing together psychology and medicine to help people sleep naturally and better, and conveys the kind of impression I want my potential clients to start building of me. I also like the nod to the symbol for balance since I use a lot of Mindfulness in my work, and I find it's a great tool for helping people to find the necessary perspective to bring their lives into better balance.

Are you getting ideas yet? If you're having difficulty figuring out where to even start with regard to defining your brand, try an exercise that social media guru Kristen Lamb has authors do in her 2013 book *Rise of the Machines: Human Authors in a Digital World*. She encourages her readers to brainstorm a word cloud, or a list of words to describe themselves, to build the basis of an engaging bio that will become the foundation of their author brand. Rather than limiting themselves to boring (my word, not hers) descriptors, she encourages them to focus on things that produce some sort of emotion like favorite foods and songs.

My take would be to think about what makes you excited about your practice. Go ahead and write out as much as you can think of. Don't worry about grammar or punctuation. You can use words and phrases. Once you get your business going, what will you be most proud of accomplishing? Think of the smiles on your clients' faces when they're in that last session and what you will have done to help them get there. Do you see yourself as a more dynamic (as in active, not psychodynamic) practitioner or a more laid-back one? You might want to choose colors that match that perspective. What are some symbols that reflect your therapeutic philosophy? Push a little and go beyond the cliché and overdone, or encourage your designer to make suggestions. Do you have a favorite color or color palette? I've always been a fan of jewel tones.

When it was time to design my logo, I wanted something that bridged the sleep world and the psychological world. Many sleep practices have a yin/yang motif with night and day as the two elements, so I knew I wanted something similar with the addition of an element to represent the psychological side. I told my graphic designer I wanted a vine or plant element since psychologists are all about growth, and she came up with my logo, which I love. She went beyond the dots in the yin and yang to put a sunrise in one half, and the simple vine I had envisioned is a robust, healthy plant that's not constrained by the symbol. The colors are a mix of bright and somber, and I think they portray the right energy for what I do.

Note—don't be seduced by a logo design that's so obscure no one will get it. Also make sure it truly reflects your practice and what you do. Then be consistent. Use the colors in the logo on your website, and if it contains words, match the fonts on all of your materials, which we'll talk about in the next section.

Marketing Materials

So now that you've figured out your branding and hopefully have gotten some help with your logo, what can you apply it to? As I mentioned, you need something to leave behind when you go on a marketing visit. You also need something to carry with you in case you get into a conversation about what you do. One of the unfortunate realities of doing interesting clinical work is that you'll end up at a party, and you'll get in *that* conversation. You know the one—where the last thing you want to talk about is work, but someone is angling for free advice. If it's someone you don't have to worry about having a dual relationship with, you can potentially escape by handing them a card and telling them you'd love to continue the conversation at your office. Hint—they probably won't call you, but there's a chance they could pass your card along to someone they know or, even better, to their physician.

Also, random aside, whenever someone has attempted the, "Oh, no, I should be careful what I say around a therapist" joke, I'll either say, "Don't worry, you're not that interesting" or "I only work if I'm getting paid."

That brings me to the first and most necessary marketing item—the business card. At the very least, the card should have your name, practice name, telephone number, and address. Mine also has my fax number for those referrals, website, and logo. All of this is on the front. I have two versions of my business card, one of which I give to patients at the end of their appointment. It has an appointment reminder template on the back that allows me to circle the day of the week and note the time and date. The other version is my marketing card, and on the front I've replaced the website with my email, and on the back I have the website and a few pithy statements about my practice. That way referral sources can remember who I am and what makes my practice unique.

Many therapists do fine with only business cards. I did for a long time. They're a very efficient way to convey the basic necessary information, and many people will look up your website or other info online. But, as you know, some people don't want to bother taking that extra step to get on the computer. And how often do you wish you didn't have to have the same conversation repeatedly? Once I'd been in practice for a little while, my main referral source asked me to put together an info sheet so he wouldn't have to explain what he knew about my practice to every patient he wanted to refer. A colleague turned this information into a brochure, which is still one of my best leave-behinds. It's bigger and harder to lose than a business card and gives a lot more info. You still have to be concise, but it's very effective. It also has pictures of my practice's providers in it.

As for other paper materials, I mentioned the referral form in the last section, and I've included a sample at the end of this chapter that you can use to build your own. They're the best kind of marketing—something that makes it easy for people to refer to you. You'll also want printed letterhead that has the look and feel of your practice logo. As I mentioned above, whenever someone sees something from your practice, it needs to have a consistent look.

Beyond what I've described so far, you can be as plain or as fancy as you want. This is a good time to bring your personality into your marketing strategy and ponder what sort of fun thing you can give to your targets, especially since the restrictions on what pharmaceutical companies can give them get tighter. Yes, big pharma is leaving a vacuum for pens and notepads. Whatever you do, make sure you're excited about whatever you're giving out. One thing that the failed marketing person did was insist that I pay for sticky notes with a faded logo in the background, my name printed on the top, and my phone number on the bottom. These went over somewhat well, although I still have a bunch of them several years later. They were a good idea, but being a creative person (at least I think so), I wasn't really excited about them or, quite honestly, the person who suggested them. I'll talk more about her later. How passionate could one be about sticky notes, right? But I really like the cool pens I bought on special about a year ago. I think the sticky note people sold my information to a bunch of other vendors, and National Pen sent me a sample pen, which I loved. Since I'm a writer, I'm picky about my pens, and that one wrote beautifully, so I got excited about it. I've shied away from paper products, but man, I love those pens, and people will be happy if you give them a gift you're excited about. I got a version of the same pens with the rubber tips for screens for my fiction marketing.

A couple of the other providers in town send out postcards periodically to a large mailing list to remind people they're there and what their specialty is. One of them, Robin Day, whom I interviewed for the book, does Dialectical Behavioral Therapy groups as her primary practice activity (R. Day, personal communication, January 13, 2017). She sends out postcards a few times a year, and guess who I immediately think of when I need to send someone for DBT? It's also very easy to hand the patient the postcard since I know I'll be getting another one soon.

As you can guess, the costs for these items can add up quickly, so you have to shop smart. Often these companies will send you samples with a limited time offer for them at half the regular price. I stocked up on the pens and haven't had to reorder yet. I also make sure to limit the number of pens I give out, usually just to the providers, so they've lasted a while. As for items like business cards and letterhead, pick a vendor, get signed up for their mailing list, and shop during sales. Personally, I like Vistaprint, but there are others, too.

I've given you the basics, so now get creative and think about fun things that you can give out that reflect your personality and practice. This is particularly important if you're using your name as your business name, so people will associate you with your specialty. One example of a very cute and clever marketing item is the stress balls from the Anxiety and Stress Management Institute. I've just come up with a sleep-related idea for my practice that I'm still playing around with and can't wait to start giving out. Are you a neuropsychologist? Can you design something brain-themed? Is health psychology more your thing? Maybe something with a heart or other health tie-in would work for you. Couples' therapist? You could give out mini voodoo doll kits. Okay, I'm kidding about that last one, but you get the idea. Play with it. Talk to family and friends. Once you build a nice list of referral sources, you can come up with something really fun and special for your best ones.

Who to Approach

The first marketing mistake many practitioners make is to engage in the inefficient strategy of direct-to-consumer marketing, or trying to attract clients directly from the general population. Even if you target a certain segment, it can be a challenge. This is an inefficient method for two reasons. First, it can cost a lot of money. Every time I've taken out an ad, it's been several hundred dollars. The only consumer advertising site that has come close to returning the investment is Psychology Today (www.psychologytoday.com), and I suspect that's because the people who read it are already interested in psychological principles and are thinking about how those principles could be applied to them. There's also a benefit to having my website linked from Psychology Today, which is that having that link from a high-traffic site gives me a boost in search engine results.

Second, there's the time cost. Taking out ads aren't so bad for time—you buy them, design them, and then forget about them until you get the next bill—but doing things where you're trying to meet potential clients face-to-face can require commitments of several hours. I did a couple of health fair-type things when I was starting out but without any benefit. It surprised me since I had worked for a chiropractor in graduate school, and he'd gotten lots of new patients from fairs. Then when I was working for a sleep disorders center, I'd do the same. I suspect that the difference is that the chiropractor and sleep disorders people could do free screenings, and we ethically have to be very, very careful about such things. Without something to hook people in, it's difficult to stand out from the crowd. Even when my former marketing person (more about her later) set up a lecture to a small group at a large employer here in town, I didn't get a single client out of it.

I'm not saying to never do talks or health fairs. Just make sure they have a larger purpose, like helping out an organization or for professional goodwill. I do a talk annually to patients at one particular clinic at Emory. I've never gotten a client from them, but since I have a professional affiliation with the university, I'm happy to give back.

Remember, our time and our money are valuable. It's best to spend them in efforts that will pay off exponentially. The best way to do this is to approach the providers who will send the clients to see us. If you think about it, it's the most efficient way to market your practice because for a finite amount of time and effort, you're increasing your potential exposure to more than one client. As one colleague pointed out, he makes up the cost of bringing lunch in one to two visits from just one client referred. If you're in a group practice or can find another way to team up with another provider, you can split costs and get even more return on your investment. This is also a good way to build relationships with colleagues.

How to Approach

If you're serious about starting your own practice, you're probably doing so partially because you like to have control over what you do and how you do it. Approaching referral sources can feel like walking up to the gatekeepers of a treasure filled castle armed only with your wits and a paintbrush. It's a loss of control. Remember—you know what you do, and you're the best one to talk about what makes your practice interesting or unique.

Like you, I was never taught anything about marketing in graduate school, so my first lessons came on the job from watching pharmaceutical reps. Okay, that's not entirely true. I've learned other things since those early days when I worked in a medical practice and would watch ridiculously good-looking people come in and chat with the staff while they waited for the physicians to have a few minutes to talk to them. As the non-prescribing provider, I wasn't of much interest to them, but they were always friendly to me. Once I sat back and thought about it, I realized there's a reason why these individuals tend to be very well-paid, especially if they're really good. In short, they know what they're doing.

First, consider the approach. It was rare for a drug rep to come in empty-handed. The ones with the bigger budgets would bring lunch for the office, which was about twenty people. If they didn't have money for a meal, they'd provide a dessert or a box of cookies or something else edible. The reps who didn't have food would still bring pens or notepads or something they could leave behind so the memory of their visit wouldn't fade as soon as they walked out the door.

Second, the genuineness, or at least the perception of such. I suspect that most of these individuals are extraverts and thrive on talking to others, but they made a genuine effort to know their targets. It was interesting to observe how they would ask about employees' and physicians' family members, coo over baby pictures, and share their own relevant parenting experiences. They approached as friendly, caring individuals, not salespeople.

Third, the knowledge. There's a reason these reps often only have one or two medications they sell. They were ready to pull out research and answer questions, and they knew their products backwards and forwards. Again, though, they didn't really do a lot of talking about their drugs. It was all about the relationships.

When I first started approaching potential referral sources, I didn't have a great budget. Or, to be honest, any budget. So I called around to different physicians' offices in the areas and tried to set up meetings with providers. Some had heard of me from my work prior to striking out on my own, but I was mostly a new name requesting a provider's time. I thought that offering a greatly needed service—nonpharmacological treatment for insomnia—would make them excited to meet with me since many physicians are uncomfortable prescribing hypnotic medication. I didn't understand until I got to be a busy provider and people wanted to meet with *me* to offer *their* services that these meeting requests can be annoying. Think about it—you have an intense day dealing with lots of distressed people who want something from you. If you're not catching up with paperwork in your downtime, you just want a chance to breathe and relax, not meet with yet someone else who's trying to get something from you. Even if you feel that providing a referral outlet for difficult patients with _____ problem is helping them, the provider may not feel that way at noon on a hectic Tuesday. Or Thursday. Or any other day ending in y.

That's the first lesson of marketing—you have to make it worth *their* time to talk to you. If it's your first visit, bring something for not just them, but their staff. Many medical practices have a rule that you can't only bring lunch for the doctors, you have to feed the rest of the staff as well. And that's actually a good thing. If a nurse or medical assistant likes you, they may be more likely to jog the doctor (or nurse practitioner or physician assistant)'s memory that you're there and treat just the problem the patient is having. Front office staff will be more likely to send along the referral or even take the extra step and call your office directly to set up an appointment.

That brings me to the second lesson of marketing to referral sources—make sending clients to you as easy as possible. A couple of years after I started my practice, I hired a marketing person to help me build referrals. I'll talk about why that didn't work out so well later, but the one good thing that came of it was that I now have a referral form for my practice. This is a sturdy—made of plastic, not paper—and easily copyable form that I give their office. It has places for the patient's information on it as well as options to check off what they're being referred for. The practice fills it out, faxes it over, and my office calls the patient to make the appointment. This works out well because it avoids the problem of potential clients receiving a card and then putting off calling to make an appointment. It also allows me to know what the referring provider had in mind when they sent the patient. The instructions on the referral form also prompt the office staff to send the patient insurance information and physician's note. Do they? Sometimes, and when they do, it saves my staff time going back and forth with the patients.

The next lesson is to try to help them like you're asking them to help you. Your best referral sources will likely become mutual ones, where you send them patients as well. Patients will sometimes ask me if I know a good primary care doc or _____ specialist, so I keep a list. One way to figure out who to approach is to have a place on your initial paperwork for patients to indicate who their primary care doctor is and to get permission to send them a letter and a short summary of the initial visit. Many physicians will be more likely to entertain the possibility of talking to you when you already have a mutual patient you've talked to them about or at least sent them information on.

Following from the idea of mutual referrals, when you speak to potential referral sources, find out about their practices. This is where our training as psychologists can be really helpful because we draw people out and get them to talk about themselves on a daily basis. If you think about it, we're the exceptions in that we don't like talking about ourselves. Most people do, especially if they're the owner or founder of the practice because they're proud of their business. Or their work if they're not an owner or founder. Inviting someone to talk about their passion is a great way to make a positive connection.

Once a referral source has sent me a client, I write a thank you note by hand and send them another card inside it. If the patient gives me permission, I also make sure the office staff sends notes to keep the referring physician in the loop. Sometimes that's all it takes to cement a referral relationship because physicians sometimes have the expectation that when they refer a client to a mental health provider, they'll never hear anything again. Remember, you're both on the same side and want the same thing for the patient, and they like it when you act as a team member. Another thing I've learned—okay, was drilled into me by a well-meaning practice manager—is that some physicians perceive a "fine line" between your degree and theirs. In other words, a few feel they're in the superior position. And alas, for our own egos, they are, since you're requesting for them to send business to you.

I'm not at all suggesting with any of this that you should be insincere, and please don't think that you're selling out, or worse, lying about your practice. Just as with therapy clients, you'll get along better with some referral sources than with others, and that's okay. At the end of the day, they're people who, like you, want the best for their patients, and that's something to connect with.

Networking Strategies

If marketing is the most dreaded word for a psychologist, networking has to be a close second. Again, you may picture yourself in a high-pressure situation where you have to present your best self while trying to figure out how to juggle your business card, a cocktail napkin full of hors d'oeuvres, and a glass of wine. And that's for the events where you're lucky enough to get a glass of wine.

Tip—always carry cash to networking events. Cash bars are ubiquitous, and ATM fees are high, especially in hotels.

Think about it for a second, though. You've already done just fine with networking without realizing it. Do you chat with the people you sit next to at continuing education events? At conferences, do you converse with people sessions you attend or alumni of your graduate program? If you're not one to strike up conversations, do you at least respond when people talk to you?

If you answered no to any of the questions in the above paragraph, you may need to rethink the private practice thing. Seriously.

In a 2010 article for the online site Entrepreneur, business expert Dan Schwabel identified four "rules of networking," which we as psychologists should excel at. The first is mutualism, which he refers to as needing to "create win-win relationships" (Schwabel, 2010). Yes, that's another cringeworthy term, but as mental health professionals, we're pretty aware of uneven balances of power, or we should be, according to our ethics codes. When networking, you're connecting for both your and the other person's good, and neither should come away with more than the other. Schwabel's second rule is giving. That's approaching the other person with the mindset of "how can I help them?" rather than "how can they help me?" and offering before requesting a reciprocal benefit. We'll talk about rule three, targeting, below, but then there's reconnecting. In other words, don't do what everyone does and let those business cards sit idle after conferences. There should be some sort of follow-up so people remember you.

Remember—it's all about making connections, and again, psychologists love information, and we're really good at getting it from people. It's also easy to convey information we're excited about. Think about networking as being a way to discover interesting things about others. That's one aspect I love about my clinical work—getting to know that the straight-laced computer guy races fancy cars on the weekend or that the proper older Southern lady secretly loves erotica novels. Networking gives you the opportunity to use your skills to uncover others' passions and how those interests are connected to their business.

But what if you're not that interesting? Well, first, I think you're selling yourself short. Everyone is interesting. Even if you don't want to talk much about yourself, you're already able to steer the conversational flow to allow the other person to talk more. I suspect that most of us are of the personality type to not enjoy small talk. Luckily we've got the skills to move past it quickly.

One principle I've carried from the writing world is that it's necessary to have an elevator pitch. If you're not familiar with the term, it's a brief nugget about your practice that can be expressed in a minute or less. Mine is, "I'm a clinical health psychologist who helps people sleep without medication and address other psychological and health problems through treatments that are supported by research. I also give talks on sleep and other psychological topics to groups and write fiction." You'll have the opportunity to come up with your own elevator pitch with the worksheet at the end of the chapter.

Between you and me, I don't mind networking, but it wears me out. Also, I get more nervous talking to other therapists than I do anyone else. I recently did a workshop on Cognitive-Behavioral Treatment for Insomnia for my state association, and that morning, my stomach was a mess. I suspect I was remembering anxiety from graduate school and all of the evaluative situations there. I had to keep reminding myself that I was the expert in the room. When it comes to your practice, you're the expert because it's your creative project, so you know more about it than anyone else. And if the person you're talking to knows more about an aspect of it like business or marketing, it's a great opportunity to learn. You won't look stupid if you ask questions, and you'll seem especially charming if you thank them for sharing a piece of knowledge you didn't have. Since therapists like to help people, we may have trouble accepting help, but if you put it in the context of making a connection, it may become easier. It's freeing to not always be the expert, and you're giving the other person an opportunity to show what they know, which will feel good to them.

So, where does one find networking opportunities? Unfortunately, aside from continuing educational events and conferences, many professional associations don't provide a lot of opportunities. You may need to look outside the field of psychology. Let me clarify—you will need to look outside the field, but do so strategically. That's where the third rule of networking, or targeting, comes in. The more picky you are about who you network with, the less time you'll waste.

If you're starting a practice, you're going to be part of the business world. Doing so may not translate into referrals, but there are other ways it can help. For example, many of the resources I consulted for this book came from connections I've made through the Georgia Romance Writers and the Atlanta Independent Women's Network. I've also had the opportunity to speak for meetings and at conferences as a result of my involvement in these organizations. Yes, non-therapy revenue-generating activities are good things. They've also allowed me to present myself as an expert, which may translate into referrals and other opportunities in the future. One of my mentors once described marketing as being like rain on a roof. Those individual drops may not seem to make much difference, but put together, they can form a stream.

You want to find organizations with people you have something in common with, so think about your interests outside of psychology. The concept of extra-professional interests seems to be easier for those who are not in academia, although there are exceptions. For example, my major professor loved photography, and he did some beautiful work. As a fiction writer, I have plenty of potential clubs and groups to join. There will be people in those groups who have outside interests as well, so they may be good resources for you. Tyra Burton, who is the subject of Box 7.1, is a colleague of mine from the Georgia Romance Writers and a professor of social media and marketing at Kennesaw State University.

Gentlemen, you may skip this paragraph if you like. Women have been noticing that in the business world, there can be a good ol' boys' network of men who help each other and their protégés along. So women have been forming networking groups to do the same for each other. I belong to two, a paid one called the Atlanta Independent Women's Network, which is comprised of female business owners, and an informal one started by one of my Facebook friends, composed of mostly business owners but also professionals who are looking to become more entrepreneurial. That one's mostly focused in the area of town I'm in, although we have members from all over. I've gotten to sponsor meetings at each, which means my business gets more exposure, and I've connected with some great ladies who have fantastic ambition and ideas. I also love the support I've gotten from members of these organizations. For example, after I moved into my current space, I went to a holiday social for AIWN and was complaining about the lack of internet wiring. Three of the members offered me the information of IT professionals they really liked. Sometimes you don't realize what you need help with until something comes up, and it's nice to have people who understand the needs of small businesses and can refer *you* to the right people.

Okay, guys, are you still with me? Good. There are general business-related associations as well, with varying costs, obligations, and levels of formality, so you should hopefully be able to find a couple that will work for you. I was invited to join one that sounded good at first. They were very careful to only have one of each kind of professional, so that person would get all the group referrals. The problem? They met ridiculously early in the morning on a weekly basis, and members were not allowed to miss meetings. Early mornings and rigid rules are two of my least favorite things, so I declined. Often organizations will allow you to visit before you join, which is a good idea so you can get an idea of the feel and the collective personality of the group. The more you participate, the more people you'll meet, and the more it will translate into friendships and business opportunities.

And hey, if you're feeling particularly frisky, go ahead and start your own group. It's easy through Meetup or Facebook. Sometimes all it takes to bring people out is for someone else to organize a gathering, especially if there's food and alcohol. If you do, limit the time you spend on it.

Website

Whereas it may have been possible ten years ago to not have a practice website, now it's a mandatory part of business. Often it's the first impression people will have of you and your practice, so it's important to make sure it looks professional and is consistent with your brand. Yes, I'm repeating this because it's important. I recently received a great compliment, which was that my personality came through on my website. Your website is your forum where you not only get to convey information about your practice, but you don't have to be constrained by the short form of an introduction letter or brochure.

Another reason to have a website is that it's your best passive marketing tool. It hangs out there on the internet, and people searching for services like yours may come across it. It also gives you the opportunity to refer people to it to gather more information if needed.

Whatever you do with your website, make sure you have your location, contact information, and hours on the front page. Nothing turns people off from a business like a poorly designed website or one that hides important information. I can't tell you the number of times I've gotten frustrated when I've gone to a business's website to find out if they're still open, and I have to dig through all kinds of pages to find out what I need. My front webpage also has some general information, and I put announcements on it, such as when we were closed for snow a few years ago, or construction around my previous office meant one side of the drive was closed.

Kim Garst, who I mentioned earlier, identifies a blog as the second "must have" to build a successful online business. The website is the first (Garst, August 2016). This is important because it keeps the website content fresh, which helps it in search engines, and is another way to allow you to let your expertise shine and connect with potential clients. If you don't think you can keep up with a blog, you might not want to commit to keeping one. Remember, though, blog posts are typically short and therefore don't have to be complicated or fancy. They also provide content to push out to social media and a potential arena for people to interact with you.

What do you blog about? Garst has a whole strategy for generating ideas that you can check out if you like, but I'm guessing you can come up with some of your own. Think about the questions your clients ask repeatedly or misconceptions you constantly have to correct. Or maybe there's a news story in your subject area to comment about or a potential seasonal or holiday tie-in. If you're getting ideas now, I encourage you to sit down and write them out before you lose them. You don't have to blog often. If you start just a few times per month as you get going, that's fine. It's also an area you can have students or trainees help you with.

Another necessary website page is your "About Me" or bio page. Can you use some of the ideas you generated with your word cloud in the branding section of this chapter to come up with an engaging but professional bio? This is also a great place to link to articles you've written or places where you've been interviewed in the media. It's important to have a good picture because people, being people and therefore sometimes shallow, will want to know what you look like. One resource I met through a networking group is a fantastic professional photographer, so I used her for my most recent head shots both for my fiction author persona and my professional one. It's totally worth it to get professional photos done, and almost as worth it to get your makeup done as well. If you're going to spend the money, you want the pictures to be good. A professional photographer will also be able to do touch-up work on the photos and get them to you in the right digital formats for website, media, and other uses.

Since you are a business, it's a good idea to have a page outlining your fees and financial policies. Mine are included in the new patient paperwork, which can be downloaded, printed out, and filled out before session. I would like at some point to have forms that people can submit directly to me, but that involves a HIPAA-compliant level of security, so it hasn't happened yet. It's very important to keep this updated. That's a reminder to myself as well.

Beyond those, other pages are optional. Since my specialty is very specific, I have a Frequently Asked Questions page that gives more information about what I do. This is also an opportunity to include information that may keep you from spending time on the phone answering the same questions repeatedly. Some therapists also have contact pages, but again, you need to be aware of confidentiality concerns.

I've listed the websites of the therapists I interviewed for the book in Appendix 2, so you can have plenty of examples while you're building your own. It can be helpful to give your web designer examples of what you like and don't like so they'll know how to start.

Social Media

Speaking of confidentiality and complications, what about social media? I'm going to assume that you know what I'm talking about, but if you're confused about what Facebook and Twitter are, I encourage you to read the 2010 article I have referenced by Dr. Keely Kolmes, who is also the co-author of *The Paper Office for the Digital Age*. She covers the basics beautifully as well as some of the pitfalls.

If you're a human in the twenty-first century, chances are that you're on social media. Many people have a Facebook profile so they can share updates with and read "news" from friends and family. Others post pictures on Instagram or engage in short-form opining on Twitter. And at this point, what professional doesn't have a LinkedIn profile? If you don't, don't feel bad—I resisted LinkedIn for a long time. The problem is that if we're in that virtual world, our clients are possibly going to come across us. I don't know how, but former patients keep finding me on LinkedIn, or LinkedIn keeps suggesting them to me. I don't know how the connections keep being made considering I don't allow the site access to address books, but it keeps happening.

This is one area where I got a lot of conflicting advice about the best role of social media in a therapy practice. Eric Marine, who is the Vice President of Claims and Risk Management for the American Professional Agency (disclosure—that's who I get my insurance from), says,

> And as far as social media, you're playing with dynamite. The purpose of social media is social. You're talking about professional. You put yourself on social media and try and go that route, which I know everybody is doing... I tend to think you open yourself up to a whole lot of stuff you don't really want unless you have very strict controls over who gets on your site, or who gets to talk with you, or who gets to comment about you. Because believe me, you don't want one of your college friends with a picture of you when you're 18 at your first beer party posting this for a laugh. Because, again, remember it's social media, you're professional... it's just a very dangerous place to be. You

have to have strict controls on it, because if you don't, that picture from 20 years ago, which was funny that night, is not going to be funny when you're trying to maintain your professional reputation.

(E. Marine, personal communication, January 5, 2017)

Marine makes a very good point—whatever you do, keep your personal and professional social media accounts separate. And if you're going to use social media in a professional sense, it's important to be aware of why you're doing so. If it's primarily to connect with potential clients, you may want to rethink your strategy unless you're targeting an age group like millennials who use that as their primary online forum.

If you do venture into the online waters, do so with intention and strategy. Think about it for a minute. Let's say one of your followers wants to come see you for therapy because you're in the same area, and they like what you tweet. Are you going to unfollow them and ask them to unfollow you when you start seeing them to avoid a potential dual relationship? That could be awkward. You could possibly work something out, but you don't want to make life more complicated than it needs to be. However, if you're going to stick to sharing news articles and talking with other providers in a professional way, a client following you may not be so bad. It's a form of online networking, and let's be honest—you shouldn't say anything online that you wouldn't say in front of a client, anyway.

I'm not saying to not "do" social media as a professional. It can be a great way to connect with other mental health professionals. You just want to be careful about it. Also, like blogging, social media requires regular updates, which takes time.

As Dr. Kolmes (2010) mentions in her article, having a professional Facebook page may not be the best way to go since you have to moderate discussions, and there's no way to block people who like the page from seeing other people who like the page. One of my former office managers set up a Facebook page for my practice, but I haven't done anything with it, and I suspect it's been so inactive for so long that no one's going to find it. I have considered, however, starting a Twitter account for myself as a professional since I'm trying to increase my speaking and business coaching services. And, now that I've talked to Tyra Burton (see Box 7.1), I'm reconsidering the Facebook page. Perhaps I'll use it to share articles and practice updates but not allow comments. I'll also put something on there that follower identities cannot be held confidential.

One area where I don't connect with current or former patients is LinkedIn. As I mentioned, I avoided LinkedIn for a long time. However, I'm going to become more active on it, again for the purposes of branding and establishing expertise. This isn't an area where I expect to find clients, but I do hope to have more indirect benefit through referrals from other professionals and to build my platform for speaking and writing. There are groups for professionals to join, so again, it's an opportunity that could work well if you're not into face-to-face networking.

To Hire or Not to Hire

In my first job out of graduate school, I was sometimes tasked with going to events like practice open houses or with visiting physicians on my own to market the sleep lab. I was the clinical director, so it made sense, but it took a lot of time, and I really didn't like it. While it was my job, I was still early in my career and didn't understand exactly what I was doing, so before I got practiced at it, marketing felt weird and awkward. I only knew that the first time I had to approach a physician on my own, I was terrified. I don't know what I was so frightened of, only that I had to do something outside of my usual realm of activities. During the course of my employment, I made several such forays, and all of them but one went off without incident. I'll tell you about that one later.

Fast forward to about a year into my practice. I was still in touch with some of my former colleagues, and at lunch one day, one of them mentioned that they had started using a marketing firm. I guess they decided that physician time was better spent seeing patients and generating revenue, so they'd hired someone to market for them. I happened to know that the senior partners didn't like to spend money, so I was intrigued. My colleague highly recommended the organization and later made an email introduction. I agreed to meet with the woman who was in charge of it. Let's call her ML for Marketing Lady.

I wish I could remember that first meeting. The fact that I don't means that it must have gone well and that I either dismissed or missed any red flags that may have popped up. I don't remember really liking ML, but I didn't dislike her. I guess her marketing strategy for herself was effective. Her services were a little pricey, but I figured that if the senior partners at my former employer thought her services were worth using, there must be something to her.

That was my first mistake.

And that brings me to my first lesson—go with your gut before hiring someone to do your marketing for you. They're going to be representing you, so you need to like them and feel that you "click." Lukewarm positive feelings aren't good enough. Request more than one meeting before hiring someone, and be very clear about the impression you want them to give and how. Remember your branding—they're going to be giving potential referral sources the first impression of your practice. It feels so silly to talk to people about what you want them to wear, but as you can see, if you don't, you don't know what will happen. When you interview them, have them describe how they see your practice and its feel, and then make sure you agree before they start representing you to anyone else.

I signed the contract, and we agreed to meet monthly to get things going. She suggested I write a template for a letter I could send to physicians and gave me an example of a referral form to use for my own. These were good and useful steps, and I still use those materials. She wanted to charge me extra to design a brochure for me, which I declined to do. I wanted to see a return on what I was already paying her before I gave her any more money. That was a smart move.

The more often I encountered ML, the more I realized her style did not at all reflect me or my personality. The most glaring example—she had a fascination for animal print clothing. I'm not talking subtle animal print, either. This was full-color stripes, spots, and more stripes. She even had one dress that started zebra at the shoulder and somehow transformed and ended with leopard print on the bottom hem. I said something to her a couple of times, how I would prefer her to dress more conservatively when she represented my practice, but she didn't listen. She'd tone down her wardrobe for one visit, but then at the next would return to her previous sartorial stretches.

Another thing I figured out was that she was marketing my practice the same way she would a medical practice. To save me some money—or to save herself some effort—she would market my practice alongside my former employer's. That meant she was likely not emphasizing what makes a mental health practice appealing, and I wonder if mine suffered in comparison due to limited insurance coverage and other factors. She also didn't research areas where the insurances I take were prevalent. I remember one lunch meeting she set up at a place near downtown Atlanta, where they had one prevalent insurance in their patient population. Was I in-network for this insurance? Nope.

ML and her son did the lunch catering for their visits, and I doubt she asked people what they wanted. For example, she brought baked fish to one visit. I'm super picky about fish, and I know a lot of other people are, too. Plus, even when it's well-cooked, it will smell, well, fishy. Hardly anyone came by, and I didn't get a single referral from that practice.

Second lesson—don't hire someone unless they have a proven record of success with marketing mental health practices. And make sure you have metrics in place to show that they're actually doing their job. They need to check in with you to see if anything they're doing is effective. ML did not.

I stupidly didn't inform her she was failing miserably at promoting my practice, so I'm definitely partially to blame.

I realize I must sound like I'm complaining a lot. I tried to be patient, and I recognize that with some marketing strategies, you need to give them six to twelve months before you see a return on your investment. However, when you've marketed to several practices, and you haven't gotten a single referral, it's time to change strategies. She didn't have any other strategies, and so I fired her at the end of the contract. By that time I was so fed up and furious with the whole situation, I couldn't even be myself when I went on lunch visits with her.

In short, if you're going to hire someone to market for you, here's what they need to demonstrate:

1. Previous success with marketing mental health practices and references who are willing to vouch that the marketing firm can do so.
2. Good understanding of your practice and if you take insurance. They need to have proven strategies for marketing mental health practices that do and do not take insurance.
3. Understanding of your personality and respect for the impression you want to convey.
4. A plan for checking in and making sure that what they're doing is effective.

My Marketing Mishap

If you're enthused about marketing your practice and have some ideas, you can skip this part. For those of you who are still so anxious about marketing and self-promotion that you'd rather go hide under your bed with the dust bunnies—or dust kitties, as we call them in my house—the following story is to encourage you. I'm going to relay an embarrassing incident that happened to me while I was out marketing with a colleague of mine. Unfortunately, said colleague was also a gossip, so not only did the incident happen, but the next day *everyone* in the practice knew about it. Here's my sad tale.

It was October many years ago, and my colleague Handsome Henry and I were sent to one of the professional buildings attached to a hospital just outside of the city to reconnect with referral sources and meet with some new ones. I've designated this colleague Handsome because he is, so much so that his likeness is on the cover of a romance novel. One of his friends was an author and was so inspired that she used him as a cover model.

I was wearing what I referred to as one of my "marketing shirts," a cute fitted long-sleeved shirt that wasn't low-cut but did have an open neckline.

Many women's shirts have a button placed right over the bosom. Typically the button placement wouldn't have been an issue, but this particular October I had gained a little weight from the combination of the age thirty metabolism slow-down and the stress-eating I'd been doing since one of my cats had been diagnosed with cancer the previous spring. I'm actually writing this on the anniversary of the kitty's passing. The shirt seemed to fit just fine, but like me, that button was struggling more than it let on.

The long afternoon turned into early evening, and as we waited in the final office to be admitted, I grumbled to my colleague that maybe I should undo the top button, and we'd get a better response. He laughed and assured me that visiting physicians' offices had variable success, so I shouldn't worry about it. We got called back to talk to the physician in his private office, and sat down. I thought I felt a draught of cold air on my chest. As Henry talked to the other doctor, I looked down and almost gasped with horror.

Yep, the button had given up. I wasn't sure how much the physician across me could see, but it was definitely more than I wanted him to.

Being a redhead, I promptly blushed with my entire body and tried to fumble with the button, which of course made the problem more obvious. Thankfully Henry, being the charming professional he was, ignored me and continued the conversation. I couldn't get the shirt to close, so I just had to sit there, blushing, hanging out, and mortified until we left.

Henry, of course, thought it was hilarious, especially since we'd just been talking about the shirt before we went in. I rebuttoned and begged him not to tell anyone. He thought it was too funny, so of course by the next day everyone knew about it. And I got comments. And it was a while before people started to forget The Button Incident.

With my cat's illness, I didn't focus on the Incident for too long, but it was a while before I wore a buttoned shirt on a marketing visit. I still continued to do the marketing—it was part of my job—and after that, it actually got easier. If I could survive my shirt trying to come off, I figured I could deal with office staff that ignored me or physicians that weren't enthused about seeing me. I also learned the "get them to talk about themselves" strategy from Harry, and it proved to be very useful in the future.

Conclusion

As you can see, there are plenty of opportunities to get creative with how you promote your practice at all budget levels. The basics include business cards and online networking through sites such as LinkedIn. You can build from there with face-to-face networking, visiting other practices, and designing fun materials. The nugget to take away from this chapter is two-fold. First, figure out your practice and professional identity and brand so you have somewhere to start. Second, have fun with it. Remember—you like connecting with people in a meaningful way, and you probably geek out about psychological knowledge in your area. You've got the skills, and as long as you don't cross any ethical lines (e.g., using Motivational Interviewing to sell something), you're welcome to use them.

Now let's move on to ethics, but first, complete the Branding worksheet, or at the very least start brainstorming.

Box 7.1 Interview with the Expert: Tyra Burton

I am so fortunate to know Tyra Burton, senior lecturer at Kennesaw State University. That's her official title. Those of us who know her and her work refer to her as the social media and internet guru. I'm grateful she took the time to answer my questions (T. Burton, personal communication, January 3, 2017).

At the very least, what should a private practice have in terms of internet presence?

I would say at a minimum a private practice should consider both a website and a Facebook page. Many consumers google to find information and a website can help them find out information about your business. I also suggest Facebook because it is the mass media of social media. Everyone is there, and it is a central hub of information for many people. Referrals especially can be easily made by your current patients to potential patients with both of these.

What are the basic things that should be included on a private practice website? What is the biggest website mistake you see?

At a minimum, your website should contain information about the type of practice you have, who you are (an 'about' section including others that work with your practice if appropriate), and location and hours. Also, if you take insurance or have other payment plans for those not covered, your website is a good place for this information. I also like to see some type of blog on sites that are trying to establish or grow their business.

A blog can help you with content to post on social media and it helps to keep your website fresh and up-to-date.

The biggest mistake I see, and one that can have negative effects for a practice to appear in search engine results, is having a site that is not updated. Google favors sites that are current, so updating your site on a regular basis will help you stay in Google's good graces (another thing a blog helps with). Also, make sure your contact information—particularly your phone number and address are correct on your website as well as any other site where you are listed (like review sites).

What do you recommend with regard to social media for psychologists and other allied health professionals? Also, what are the risks or things to be careful of?

Whenever you are dealing with people's healthcare information, there is a need to be aware of federal regulations about not revealing your patients' identities or history without prior approval. This can make it difficult to discuss 'success stories' but with proper permission (always have patients sign release forms before you post), you can post their stories. Also, make sure that you get photo releases, if anyone—staff included—give you the ok to be pictured on your website or on social media.

Facebook is a good starting point, and from there you can choose if any other social site makes particular sense for your target market or type of therapy. If you are using art or animals for therapy, there is the potential for visual story-telling and Instagram might be a good choice for you. If you find that you have a younger audience, you might want to consider Twitter.

For content, I would keep the 80/20 rule in mind. Eighty percent of your content should not be about you and trying to 'sell' anything. Only 20 percent of your content should be about you and selling directly. Theme days and tips connected to your practice are good ways to have content for your social platforms to fill that 80 percent of time.

Lastly, I suggest having a LinkedIn profile. LinkedIn is a network where consumers may go to find out more about your professional life. Even though I have a website, I have a LinkedIn profile that goes more in-depth into my professional background including a list of all my publications and awards. LinkedIn is a great place to establish your credibility as well as get testimonials from patients.

What is the main mistake you see our type of business make on social media?

The main mistake I see many businesses of all types making on social media is over-selling. Consumers are not on social media—for the most part—wanting to be sold on a product. If you provide useful information, you can get in their good graces and be in the consideration set if they are ever looking for the service you provide.

Is there a specific social media site that seems to be best suited for our type of business?

Facebook and LinkedIn are the two sites that are best suited to private practices. LinkedIn will highlight your professional credentials. Facebook is like the yellow pages of old in many ways. Consumers will look here for your listing and it makes it easy for people to refer you.

We hear a lot about Search Engine Optimization (SEO), and I'm often approached by companies who promise to maximize my page finds. What are some ways for us to maximize that ourselves without having to hire consultants? Related—is using Google AdWords worth it?

SEO has some key factors that have remained constant or been high-lighted by changes. Primarily, having an up-to-date website, that has fresh, relevant and valuable content for consumers will help you appear higher in search results. Also, you want to use key words associated with your practice type, but don't over-use them (keyword stuffing). Again, having your location information up-to-date is key. Google frequently returns results to consumers that are location based. If you go to Google right now and search for Veterinarian, the top results you get (after any ads) will most likely be vets that are geographically near your IP address/location. Lastly, make sure you have a responsive website. This means that your website automatically adjusts for the device that someone is using to view your website. This makes your website mobile friendly and Google greatly prefers responsive sites to non-responsive when ranking.

Google AdWords can be worth the investment if you have a new practice or have relocated. AdWords will be particularly powerful when you have a clearly defined target market (especially a niche market), and other features of your practice that makes you stand-out from the competition. One of the reasons I think it works best in niche market situation or when there are unique qualities about your practice is cost. More generic keywords or keyword groups such as 'counselor' or 'grief therapist' will have a high CPC (cost-per-click) than more specific terminology. With most service businesses, referrals rather than Google AdWords are the key way to grow your business. Make this easy for your current clients to do and find ways to reward them for helping you grow your practice.

What are some other strategies for increasing traffic to our websites? For example, I've heard that having downloadable forms will help increase ranking on Google since people will go to the website and interact with it to find them. Is that true?

Content is king. If you create engaging content that adds value for your target market, you can use that content in social media posts as well as it being found in consumer web searches. Also, I can't stress enough how important it is to have a responsive site. More and more consumers use smartphones increasingly every day.

I honestly can't speak to the downloadable forms—mostly I have heard of using them to get leads (like a whitepaper—you want to read this, well, you have to give me your email address).

Bibliography

Garst, K. (August 30, 2016). 5 "Must haves" to build a successful online business [blog post]. Retrieved from http://boomsocial.net/5-must-haves-to-build-a-successful-online-business/.

Garst, K. (December 5, 2016). 13 Common mistakes to avoid when building your online brand [blog post]. Retrieved from http://boomsocial.net/13-common-mistakes-avoid-building-online-brand/.

Kolmes, K. (2010). A psychotherapist's guide to Facebook and Twitter: Why clinicians should give a tweet! Retrieved from https://www.psychotherapy.net/article/psycho-therapists-guide-social-media.

Lamb, K. (2013). *Rise of the machines: Human authors in a digital world.* United States: WANA International.

Schwabel, D. (November 2, 2010). How to brand yourself: An introduction. Retrieved from https://www.entrepreneur.com/article/217481.

Worksheet 1—Branding and Practice Identity

One of the most challenging and also most important steps when starting a practice is defining your practice identity. On this worksheet, I'm going to (hopefully) give you some exercises that will get you thinking in the right direction.

1. The "word cloud" (à la Kristen Lamb's *Rise of the Machines: Human Authors in a Digital World*). Write out words that describe you and your practice but also invoke emotion in you.

2. Now circle the ones that evoke the strongest emotion and list them here.

3. Take the words from #2 and put them into a pithy statement about your practice. It may be similar to your mission statement, but think more about answering the question, "What kind of work do you do?" Let this be the basis for your elevator pitch. Try to stick with strong verbs that convey what you do.

4. Now look at the interesting words that describe you and put them together into a four- to five-sentence bio.

REFERRAL FORM

Please fax this form along with office notes, patient I.D., and insurance card to XXX-XXX-XXXX

Patient Name: _____

D.O.B.: _____

Best Phone: _____ (Circle: **Home   Cell   Work**)

Okay to leave message?   Y/ N

SYMPTOMS AND HISTORY

PLEASE CHECK ALL THAT APPLY:

____ Problem 1 ____ Problem 2
____ Problem 3 ____ Problem 4

PREVIOUS DIAGNOSIS OF:

____ Anxiety Disorder (Please specify): _____

____ Depression   ____ Bipolar Disorder ____ Substance Abuse

(Please specify): _____

____ Other Psychological Disorder: _____

SERVICES REQUESTED:

____ (Type of) Evaluation   ____ Treatment 1
____ Treatment 2   ____ General Psychological Evaluation
____ General Psychotherapy

Provider Name   Provider Signature

Date

Office Contact   Phone

Contact Email

Let's Get Ethical

8

Ethics is an area my state association has us do continuing education activities in regularly. The current rule is six hours per two-year licensing cycle. I can see why—it's good to know the rules and the tools for protecting our clients and ourselves. Since you likely got ethics training in graduate school and there are other resources out there, I'm going to just hit the basics. Box 8.1 is with Eric Marine, Vice President of Claims and Risk Management at the American Professional Agency. He had a lot of great perspectives I'm excited to share with you.

Let's go ahead and talk about the American Psychological Association's ethical principles and discuss generally how they can apply to business practices (American Psychological Association, 2017). We'll get more into specifics with applicable standards later in the chapter. If you've been out of school for a while, you may, like me, not have reviewed them, so let's do so now. If you're not a psychologist and have your own profession's ethical code, I encourage you to review it at this time because there's going to be overlap.

Principle A: Beneficence and Nonmaleficence

Basically, this is our correlate to the medical profession's "do no harm." And we certainly don't intend to, but sometimes situations come up where we may feel stuck between our ethical code and the law. For example, let's say one of your patients travels to a state where you're not licensed but runs into family stress. They call you for support, but you're not licensed to practice where they are, which is a legal rule. Do you call them back and ignore the legality?

One situation I've encountered was figuring out after careful assessment that the client had a substance abuse problem. The client stated they'd been adequately treated, but after our second session ended up in the hospital for a short stay as a result of their use. It turned out they'd been lying to me about stopping. They wanted to continue therapy with me since they liked me, but treating acute substance abuse and dependence problems is outside my realm of competency. I referred the patient elsewhere, and they were angry with me, but I didn't feel like I could help them until they adequately addressed their other problem. Did their hurt feelings constitute harm?

Principle B: Fidelity and Responsibility

When clients come to us, they're in a very vulnerable position. They're going to bare their souls and reveal their weaknesses in order to resolve whatever they're coming in for, and it's our responsibility to respect that we have an advantage over them. This is where dual relationships come into play. We need to avoid dual relationships as much as possible, but sometimes it's difficult. For example, what if a referral source has heard such great things about you that they want to come see you as a therapist? This situation can feel tricky because you don't want to anger them and make them stop referring to you, but you don't want to risk subjecting them to undue influence to continue referring to you. Or what if they don't have a good therapeutic experience with you? Will that damage your business? The obvious answer seems to be not to see them, but what if you're the only one with your specialty in the area? There's also the fact that in the medical community, dual relationships aren't an issue. Physicians frequently treat each other and each other's family members, so they may have the same expectation of you.

This is also the main ethical principle that applies to doing pro bono work, but what does that mean, exactly? Do you see people for free? Charge a greatly reduced rate? But what does that mean for your insurance contracts?

Principle C: Integrity

This one basically says not to lie. At first glance, it seems to apply mostly to the research world, where some deception may be a necessary part of psychological experiments. I certainly had it as part of my dissertation, which used a modified form of the Taylor Aggression Paradigm. In private practice, it's primarily applicable to business practices and therapeutic techniques. I like to assure my patients I run a "no surprises" practice when it comes to financial responsibilities, and if there's an error or confusion, I'll eat the cost. The frustration comes in when insurance companies stop paying for whatever reason. That can be a hard boundary to negotiate, especially for a less experienced therapist. As for therapeutic approaches, I use mostly empirically supported treatments, and I'm careful to alert patients when I'm about to suggest or use something that's my own development even if it's based on the same principles as the research-supported treatments.

Principle D: Justice

If you want an obvious example of a recent violation of this principle, remember the psychologists who got in trouble for advising the government on torture techniques. However, in the business world, this one is probably the most aspirational to the business of psychology. As the first sentence states, "Psychologists recognize that fairness and justice entitle all persons to access to and benefit from the contributions of psychology and to equal quality in the processes, procedures and services being conducted by psychologists." Yes, it would be great if community service boards could ensure the same quality of care as a totally self-pay private practice does so that the same level of care is accessible to everyone regardless of income level. However, if I saw most of my patients for free or greatly reduced rates, I couldn't keep my business open. This one combined with Principle B make for strong encouragement to engage in community service and pro bono work.

Principle E: Respect for People's Rights and Dignity

For those of us in private practice, this principle applies to making an effort to be aware of our own biases, as the principle states, and using that to avoid discriminating against certain populations or patient profiles. This doesn't mean we can't protect ourselves, for example, making sure we're compensated for the extra time and effort it takes to deal with the legalities of someone who's involved in a lawsuit. We also need to be aware of the need to protect our most vulnerable patients.

The overarching rule for all of the potential situations that fall under these and the standards is the need to set expectations from the beginning and to document carefully.

Challenges to Confidentiality

Sometimes the very act of doing business in a professional or office building can introduce risks to confidentiality that are impossible to anticipate. Here are some building-related situations I've encountered.

Window Washers

I've had two tenth-floor offices in my time as a private practitioner, and occasionally the buildings would hire contractors to wash the windows. Sometimes they'd give us warning, sometimes they wouldn't. If they did, I'd keep my blinds closed. If not, I'd end up scrambling to close them. I don't know how much the window washers could see through the windows, but I didn't want to take chances.

Fire Drills

Remember how when we were in school, we'd have fire drills? Apparently, office buildings have them, too, or are supposed to. And, apparently, it's legally required for everyone to participate. My last office building was full of lawyers and therapists, and one random Wednesday afternoon I was coming back from lunch when I heard the alarm and saw people coming out of the building. I recognized some of my therapist colleagues walking and chatting with people who could have been coworkers or could have been their clients. There was a possibility for either. What if your client isn't mobile or can't go down several flights of stairs? You're supposed to leave them on the landing in the supposedly fire-proof stairwell and tell the firemen that there's someone on the #th floor in the _____ stairwell. Of course, that's what you'll want to do in a real fire, but I'm not sure about a fire drill.

Oh, and it's impossible to schedule around fire drills because they're supposed to be a surprise—very annoying from a business perspective.

Repairs

Every so often in my last office building, they'd send out a message that some repair person or organization would be visiting offices on a certain set of dates to examine duct work or other random building stuff. I always made sure to tell them when to avoid my office because I had patients. Sometimes I'd have to put off repairs on my own office due to my client schedule.

If you have staff, it's important to make sure they're trained to always consider confidentiality and other applicable ethics concerns. Some office suites have a receptionist area with a window that can be closed, but most of them don't. Last week, my office manager emailed me a little after 3:00 p.m. as I reviewed that client's sleep diaries to say she would have to put off returning calls because my 4:00 p.m. patient had arrived an hour early and was just hanging out in the waiting room playing with their phone. Some therapists encourage their patients to not arrive more than five minutes early in order to avoid crossing paths with other patients or for this reason. I've considered asking people not to bring family members if they're not coming into session with them since my current waiting area is so small. If you treat several members of the same community—for example, a college or workplace—you might want to try not scheduling them back-to-back with each other. Sometimes you can't help it if clients encounter others they know, but it doesn't hurt to try to avoid that occurrence.

It can feel silly to have to spell out confidentiality policies since they seem like common sense, but you never know what people will do. I had one receptionist, whom I ended up firing, who didn't want to lick envelopes but who didn't seem to know how to use one of those envelope-moistening sticks. She tried to send out one batch of patient closing letters by moistening the very end of the envelope flap point with a wet paper towel. So now I have a policy that correspondence must only leave the office in a fully sealed box or envelope. If I were online, this is where I would insert #headdesk.

Another potentially tricky area is treating adolescents and young adults who are age 18 or less. Or those who are over 18 and who have very, let's say, involved parents. I had a recent case where a young adult had scheduled and canceled four times, twice within the 24-hour cancellation penalty window, and whose mother called and demanded they be seen. I opted not to talk to her since the patient is of adult age and I didn't have permission to talk to her. I didn't reschedule that particular patient again since they couldn't manage to come in for an initial visit.

With regard to adolescents, I copy what I learned from an earlier clinical mentor and have my office manager inform the parent, who's usually scheduling the first visit, that they'll need to come with their son or daughter for the first visit. After they arrive and do the paperwork, I'll bring the teenager and whatever parent accompanied them into my office and lay out some ground rules that everyone will hopefully agree to. I acknowledge that the parents have a legal right to the records, but I also want the son or daughter to feel comfortable being open with me. So I tell them I'll inform them if the adolescent is a danger to themselves or someone else or if they're using heavy drugs. Talk of alcohol use, marijuana use, and sexual activity stay within our confidential relationship.

Most of the adolescents are on board. As you can imagine, some parents are more comfortable with this than others. And some of them are too comfortable. One parent mentioned that their child's coach said the adolescent could call any time if they were caught in a difficult alcohol situation, and what would I recommend if her child got too drunk to drive? I think she wanted to add me to the child's list of rescue-if-drunk people, which I don't blame her for. However, I don't have kids and don't want to be responsible for anyone else's, so I said, "Call the coach."

Of course, there are times when we have to violate confidentiality, and this is spelled out in my paperwork. Ideally, you'll go over these limitations at the start of treatment, too. Yes, this is hopefully a review of what you learned in graduate school, but it never hurts to be reminded. Here are the situations:

If the client is a danger to themselves, you have to make sure they stay safe. This means assessing whether they have ideation, or thoughts about harming themselves, intent, or they clearly state they intend to do so, and a plan for doing it. If all three are present, you may need to involuntarily commit them, which means you need to be familiar with the procedures for doing so in your locality. Consider writing the instructions for involuntary commitment down, having the proper form on hand, and keeping them in a place you can get to easily. If the patient leaves your office, you still need to alert the authorities. That's one reason you get their home address. I did have one patient call me after hours—one of my two after-hours calls—and tell me they had taken a gun and driven out a country road. I talked them down, thankfully, but this incident demonstrates that at this point, psychotherapy patients are pretty savvy about what's going to get them "locked up," as they call it. There have been a few times when I suspected that the client was flirting with the idea, but they wouldn't say the "magic words" to make me have to take action. That's where the therapeutic alliance comes in. Although suicide contracts haven't been shown to be effective, if you have a strong enough relationship with the patient, sometimes them promising to contact you if they're feeling suicidal will be enough to keep them safe until the next session. This is why it's good to make sure everyone is clear on after-hours contact policies from the beginning.

If a client is a danger to someone else, you need to be familiar with the laws in your state to know what you are legally allowed to do. We all learned about the Tarasoff case in graduate school, but whether therapists are immune from prosecution for violating confidentiality to warn the intended victim or alert the authorities is different in each state. This is one of those frustrating inconsistencies we have to navigate. For example, my state of Georgia is not a Tarasoff state, so we don't have duty to warn. I've had to think a lot about it, and I have decided that if I were to encounter this situation, I would alert the authorities and document the hell out of the visit and what the client said. After trying to talk the client out of their intended course of action before violating their confidentiality, of course. I would also tell them what I intended to do.

What if a client has committed an illegal act in the past or has a family member who has? You can't do anything. I haven't yet had anyone confess to murdering someone, but plenty of people have admitted to illegal drug use. Also, if someone requests that I not add something to the record, I will ask them why and usually comply with their request or put it in vague terms that only I will understand. Again, typically it's not anything too concerning, and I do try to meet the basic requirements for therapy documentation.

If a client alerts you to elder or child abuse, there is a mandatory reporting law. Again, patients can be pretty savvy about this one and not give you enough information to report, but you have to do your best. Again, document as much detail of the conversation as you can and encourage the patient to do the right thing for the protection of the vulnerable person. I had one tricky case where I was aware of a foster child who was homosexual being placed temporarily with a foster parent who was homophobic. I had to determine whether emotional abuse was present and how long the child was in the situation. This was definitely one case where I consulted with a peer as to what I should do. Since there was no clear evidence of emotional abuse, at least not from the client's report, and the situation was very temporary, I chose not to take any action.

If a judge issues a court order for your records, you may have to comply. My recommendation is to first call your state licensing board, which will typically have an ethics consultant, and see what your recourse may be. If they say you have to turn over records, try to see if the judge will accept a written summary.

You do not have to turn over your complete records when clients are involved in lawsuits—again, unless there's a court order—or when they're applying for disability. Disability lawyers and companies will typically accept summaries, and they'll often pay for your time to write them. Back when I was starting out, I had a patient who was suing someone, and this patient wanted my records to demonstrate the emotional distress. I made the mistake of releasing the records to them. They then proceeded to review them and insist on changes. That's when I came up with my policy of only releasing summaries, and I justify it with the wording, "Since my records are written in psychological language, in which terms may have different connotations than spoken English, I only release them to other providers who are directly involved in the care of the patient." That way I can still send notes to referral sources—assuming the clients have given me permission to do so—but can keep them protected otherwise.

What is the best way to send notes to referral sources? Unfortunately, this is one area where the medical world is still stuck in the 1990s. Most offices still have a fax machine or online fax service, and that's how most of my notes go out. My EHR has the capability of faxing from within it, and for other matters, I use a HIPAA-compliant online fax service that my office manager or I will upload a PDF to. Email, being as secure as shouting across the room, is out. One referral source, who did not have a fax service, wanted me to use a shared folder in Dropbox, which is also not secure, so I ended up going really old school and mailing them. "Snail mail," being protected by the federal government, is technically also secure. Luckily I haven't had to do that too often.

Advertising Pitfalls

When I started my practice, bargain sites like Groupon and LivingSocial were hugely popular. They operate on the premise of luring people in with a discount and then giving them a good experience so they return. Several people—not psychologists—suggested I should do something like that to bring in patients. I declined. Why? Because to do so would be an ethical violation.

Let's examine the hypothetical scenario. Let's say I would do a Groupon for a free 15-minute consultation, as my dietitian colleagues do. You know as well as I do that our consultations typically last way beyond 15 minutes, so we'd have to put something in place that the meter would start at minute 16. That could get awkward and result in divided attention for everyone, which would not make for a great experience. Even if you offered a free consultation, what then? You could try to tell people they would be responsible for your visit fees on the second visit, but even if you have them sign something, many would either ignore it or expect a discount the next time. Or they would think they're getting free information and intend to not continue with you, which makes for a waste of your time and an opportunity cost because you could be spending that energy with a client who intends to follow through.

The ethical problem occurs when you hook someone into treatment you or they may not be able to continue. Consider the case of the person who wants free information about themselves. In general psychotherapy, often talking about the problem is enough to begin the therapeutic process. Assuming you're a responsible provider, you want to be able to continue, especially if there's good rapport. It may hurt a potential client more if they were to really connect with you during the screening but then not be able to follow up with you, setting up the next person they see to be the "rebound therapist." You know what I'm talking about—it's really hard to be the next therapist after the client stops seeing someone they really liked, and like a lot of rebound relationships, there's a chance it won't last long.

As I mentioned in the last chapter, sometimes mental health practitioners do screenings in situations such as health fairs or other larger efforts. The first practice situation I was in participated in a building-wide effort for National Depression Screening Day (https://mentalhealthscreening.org/programs/ndsd), which is held annually on the Thursday of the first full week of October. I didn't take part, but some of the other practitioners did. I believe they set up 15-minute time slots for people to come do and talk about the results of the Beck Depression Inventory. The point was to give the practice exposure, but also to help people who might not have known they needed help to realize they may. If you're a stages of change person, it was designed to move people from pre-contemplation to contemplation or from contemplation to preparing. The effort was ethical and worked since it was structured, and there was no assumption that they were setting up a therapy relationship. It may have even facilitated people seeking therapy since it broke down the first barrier a lot of people have, which is a negative view of mental health practitioners.

Also, when advertising, it's best to avoid promises or guarantees that our services will work. I tell my patients that the treatments I do have been shown to work for a lot of people, but I avoid use of extreme language. Yes, this seems like a no-brainer, but sometimes even well-meaning practitioners can be seduced by advertising initiatives.

As Ethical Standard 5 states, we also have to be careful about how the media presents us (American Psychological Association, 2017). This is one of those areas that can be a huge opportunity for exposure for our practices, but it's also a risky one. I've had the good fortune to consult on several articles in the popular press, but I've found that journalists will not run the article by me before it goes to press in order to make sure my comments are being presented in an accurate way and context. Now I insist upon email interviews—most of them prefer that, anyway—and I try to make what I say as clear and concise as possible so it can't be chopped apart. Remember, journalists like sound bites, so sometimes we have to play to the audience. By the way, I've never gotten a client as a result of doing a media interview, but I have all the links on my bio on my website, so I suspect they've helped to establish me as a credible expert. I'll talk more about that—and how to maintain good relationships with journalists—in Chapter 10.

I've been approached a few times by representatives of magazines or advertising outlets who put together "best of" doctor lists. Upon first impression, it sounds great, but then once you dig into it, it's not based on patient feedback, reviews, or other measures, but rather a paid advertisement. The way these things are presented to consumers, it's not always clear that it's an advertisement, which makes such situations in direct conflict of Ethical Standard 5.02 (b) "Psychologists do not compensate employees of press, radio, television or other communication media in return for publicity in a news item" and (c), which states, "A paid advertisement relating to psychologists' activities must be identified or clearly recognizable as such" (American Psychological Association, 2017). My advice—if someone calls you wanting to include you in a "Who's Who" or "Best of," decline unless it's free. If they offer to sell you something to hang on your wall, see if they'll still include you if you decline to buy the plaque or framed certificate. There are some legitimate ones, but they're the exception. For example, one of our local magazines will do a "Best Doctors of Atlanta" issue, and it's definitely for free since I had a colleague who didn't realize he'd been included until he got the banquet invitation. Be careful, and if you suspect something's fishy, don't do it. This also falls under the direct to consumer advertising I mentioned earlier, and these particular ads, even if they're clearly marked as such, tend to not be worth it because they're really expensive.

One gray area in advertising is content marketing. This is the magazine version of those sponsored tweets or Facebook posts that scroll across your news feed. The provider pays for the article to be written, and while the layout looks like a news article, it's clearly marked as sponsored content or an advertising feature. Some therapists take advantage of this opportunity, but others aren't comfortable with the possible deception. If you're considering this, take a look at such articles in that publication and see how clearly they're marked as sponsored.

There's also the current issue that the internet is a popularity contest, and sometimes potential clients will go online and look at your reviews. As mental health practitioners, this puts us in a bind because we know unhappy people are more likely to write reviews, but as standard 5.05 states, "Psychologists do not solicit testimonials from current therapy clients/patients or other persons who because of their particular circumstances are vulnerable to undue influence" (American Psychological Association, 2017). I know of one practitioner who puts postcards in his waiting room that list the sites his practice is rated on. He doesn't mention them and leaves it to the clients to pick them up and decide what, if anything, they'll do. I've tried that strategy with mixed success in that people will give the postcards to me or my office manager but won't post anything online. As for when you get negative reviews, the advice is mixed. Some professionals say not to respond, and others say to respond but in a kind, compassionate way. If you do decide you want to respond to reviews, be sure you have in your paperwork that you reserve the right to do so even if it may be a violation of confidentiality.

Paperwork Basics I

As hard as I've tried, I've still not managed to have a paperless office. That's because every time I try to reduce my new patient paperwork, another regulation comes along, or I have to include something else business-related because of situations I've encountered. For example, for my insurance patients, I now say I'll attempt to get payment from the insurance company twice, and then the patient will be responsible for the cost of the visit if the claim is denied both times.

Since you're setting up expectations at the first visit, the new patient paperwork should include policies and information applicable to your clinical work, financial policy, insurance policy (if applicable) with permission to send information to the insurance company, and informed consent to treatment. I'll briefly discuss each here.

Regarding Clinical Work and Informed Consent: The Psychological Services Agreement

Informed consent is such an important part of establishing a clear therapeutic relationship that it's mentioned several times in the ethical standards. Standard 10 goes into the most detail, and you can almost view standard a as a checklist for what needs to be included in your paperwork: "(a) When obtaining informed consent to therapy as required in Standard 3.10, Informed Consent, psychologists inform clients/patients as early as is feasible in the therapeutic relationship about the nature and anticipated course of therapy, fees, involvement of third parties and limits of confidentiality and provide sufficient opportunity for the client/patient to ask questions and receive answers. (See also Standards 4.02, Discussing the Limits of Confidentiality, and 6.04, Fees and Financial Arrangements.)"

In my paperwork, I start with an explanation of the therapeutic process and make sure the patients understand that they are in control of whether they continue therapy after the first visit. Since many of them are coming from medical practices, I clarify that they will be required to be active participants and will have "homework" between sessions. I also mention risks such as undesirable behaviors sometimes getting worse before they improve and having to face discomfort. I also mention potential benefits, but that these aren't guarantees.

Of course I give them limits on confidentiality in writing as well and indicate that their signature provides consent for me to follow them, and I do include a paragraph on if the patient should indicate they're going to harm another person. I also include my policy on preparing legal documents in this session, which is as follows:

> If you do request your information to be shared in a legal matter (e.g., Social Security Case, Workman's Comp Case prior to the claim decision, divorce or other proceedings), a charge of $185/hour will be applied for preparation of a clinical summary, as it is our policy not to share clinical notes with anyone besides other healthcare professionals. This is for your protection, as they are written in clinical, not legal language, and the information contained in them could be misinterpreted.

I do this for two reasons. First, I'm hoping to minimize records requests to only those which are necessary since it puts a burden on my office and my time. Second, I'm protective of my patients and their records. I want to be able to include relevant information in session notes so I can treat the patient, but these notes aren't for everyone to read even if I do try to follow the principle of writing them as if the patient and their attorney were standing over my shoulders. As I mentioned, our vocabulary is unique to our profession, and some terms may be misconstrued in a way that's disadvantageous to the patient.

One time when you have to release full records is when you're dealing with a Workman's Compensation case. Unfortunately, that's the only way to get paid for your work. The good thing is that you're typically releasing the records to a nurse who's managing the case and acts as a support to the patient, so the situation falls under the treating healthcare professional clause.

I also include a paragraph about patient rights under HIPAA, but I have separate policies since they're long. The patients can access my HIPAA policies on my website. This is one area where you may have to invest some money to get up-to-date ones, both to give patients and for your own office policies and procedures. If you do some digging online, you can find free policies. Otherwise, services may charge you up to a few hundred dollars. Luckily, they don't get updated that often. I get mine through Dr. Becky Beaton's online store (http://www.drbeckybeaton.com/shopping-center.html). She's the founder and director of the Anxiety and Stress Management Institute and gives ethics workshops, so I know she's credible and keeps things up to date.

I do mention billing, but briefly since that's discussed in future pages. Thanks to technology and the fact we live so much of our lives online, I've had to add an "Internet Contact" policy. It's strange how many people will try to friend me on LinkedIn in particular during or after treatment. Here are my policies:

> Social Media: We do not accept friend or contact requests from current or former clients on any social networking site (Facebook, LinkedIn, etc). Adding clients as friends or contacts on these sites can compromise your confidentiality and our respective privacy. It may also blur the boundaries of our therapeutic relationship.
>
> Email: We may occasionally email sound files for at-home practice and will always ask your consent before doing so. As email is not completely secure or confidential, we ask that you limit email contact and call the office for appointment changes or clinical questions. Please do not email content related to your therapy sessions. Any emails we receive from you and any responses that we send to you become a part of your legal record.

I'll talk more about email in a future section.

The last paragraph of the Psychological Services Agreement, in bold, states: "Please discuss any questions or concerns with your therapist. Your signature below indicates that you consent for us to treat you, that you understand and agree with the terms of the Psychological Services Agreement, and that you acknowledge receipt of the HIPAA Notice."

You have to have some variation of the statement "consent for us to treat you" for it to count as informed consent.

Financial Policy

Part of the ethics of informed consent is fees, and this is also where I discuss session length. I did have one patient who complained that he wasn't getting a full hour of my time, so I had to explain to him that a therapy hour is different from a regular hour. This is also where I make sure they see that there will be two attempts to collect payment from their insurance company. I also have my cancellation policy here, which requires 24-hour notice for Tuesday through Friday appointments and notice by 1:00 on Friday for Monday appointments. I have this policy so my office staff can have time to reach out to the cancellation list. It's also important to mention what insurance companies will and won't pay for. For example, some patients think that their insurance company will pay for a missed session, which is not the case. They also can't use their Health Savings Account or Flexible Spending card money for late cancellation or no-show fees.

Credit Card Policy

Over the past few years, I've been keeping credit card numbers on file. When you look into credit card companies, find one that will keep the numbers securely for you so that no one in your office can access them, only run them for charges. Some patients don't feel comfortable agreeing to this, so we will rarely keep a $50 check or cash in the patient's file to deposit if they cancel late or don't show. Sometimes we've had to decline to treat a patient because they won't agree to this policy, but this is also a rare case. At this point I can tell them that whenever I've made an exception, I've not gotten paid, so we don't make exceptions anymore. Most people are okay with it considering how many places require credit cards to hold appointments. It's important to assure the patient that we will do our best to contact them before running the card. Sometimes cards decline, and we can't do anything about that. I've only had a client challenge a charge twice, and I was able to work it out with the client and credit card company both times because I had a copy of the signed receipt.

This is also the section where I tell people that if they run more than 15 minutes late, we reserve the right to reschedule or abbreviate the appointment. I respect my patients' time, just as I expect them to respect mine. While I may run a few minutes late some days, I do try to stay on schedule as much as possible. You may be more flexible, which is fine. I'll admit my being strict about time comes from my employment in a medical practice, where people arriving late without paperwork would snowball into a clinic delay of an hour or more. Now that I've been on the other side of that situation, I have new sympathy for my medical providers. Since some practice managers care more about income than the provider or patient experience, they'll refuse to reschedule late people. I choose for my patients not to go through that stress, and frankly, I don't want it, either. Plus, as we learn in our training, chronic lateness can be a sign of the underlying pathology, so it's important to confront and limit that behavior as much as possible.

Patient Information

This is the sheet where the patient fills in all the information you'll need to contact them including name, address, phone, where messages can be left, sex/identified gender, marital status, employer, position, who referred them and whether we can contact and send notes to that person, whether they've been in therapy before, for what and where, emergency contact, responsible party, and primary insurance info.

Reminders

Many mental health practitioners don't do appointment reminders. Since I straddle the line between the medical and mental health worlds, I do as a courtesy to my patients. In my paperwork, I emphasize that since technical difficulties happen, it is ultimately their responsibility to keep up with their appointments whether they get a reminder or not. I have them indicate whether they'd prefer to get telephone or email reminders or no reminder at all. Some people request text reminders, which my EHR doesn't do yet.

Primary Care Physician Information

This is good information to have, both for marketing purposes and for coordination of care since often the PCP is the prescriber for hypnotic or psychotropic medication. It's good for primary care physicians to know what specialists their patients are seeing, and I do count my work on par with that of a medical specialist, not just an auxiliary healthcare provider. My view of myself as a specialist is based on my work on the cusp of sleep medicine and psychology and because I believe in the interconnectedness of mind and body, and I have no doubt that problems in one area affect all the other aspects of my patients and their lives. With that in mind, I ask patients for permission to send an introductory note with a brief visit summary to their PCP. Sometimes they decline, which is fine. Often they won't read this section closely and put their referring physician's information in. Or they'll put in the PCP info and say no, I can't send them a summary. I'll at the very least encourage them to talk to their PCP about our work together.

Paperwork Basics II

Once the patient comes in, you need to document what happened in the visit. My initial notes tend to follow a somewhat medical format since that's where I started out in my profession, but they do include most of the basic information. Here are my sections:

Presenting Problem

This is one or two sentences, usually something like, "Mr./Ms. is a [age]-year-old [race or ethnicity] [gender] who presents with [problem(s)].

History of Present Illness (HPI)

The patient's self-report of how and when the problem started and developed.

Diagnostic Interview

The problem as it manifests in the present. This is where I'll include information about current sleep schedule and medications, environment, effects, and previous attempts at addressing the presenting problem itself. For general psychotherapy clients, I have the patient describe the current problem, the symptoms (for DSM-5 diagnostic purposes), how it affects their lives, and other pertinent information *to the presenting problem.*

Social History

This is where I gather information on substance use—alcohol, caffeine, tobacco, and recreational drugs—and exercise as well as the patient's living situation including whether they're married or partnered and have children. This is also where I'll note who else lives in the household, e.g., young or adult children, elderly parents.

Medical History

Even if you're not working in health psychology, it's good to know what other problems the patients have. I have a check box field with the most common ones I hear in my clinic as well as space to notate others. I'll also include medication lists in the chart if patients bring them.

Psychological History

This field is more useful for my sleep patients, since I'll likely have covered the history in a previous section for my general psychotherapy patients.

I'll include past therapy, psych hospitalizations, and psychotropic medication history for drugs not used for sleep.

Family History

Since we know problems run in families, it's good to notate if anyone else in the family has or had a similar problem. It's also good to know if there was a history of abuse or alcoholism.

Objective

How did the client present? Were they dressed and groomed appropriately for the session? Were they on time? Was affect within normal limits or remarkable in some way? For example, sometimes clients present in a lot of distress over one problem but have very little affect evident when discussing others.

Assessment

This is my impression of what the diagnosis is and whether the patient appears motivated for treatment. I'll also include screening instrument scores. If you don't have an EHR, you'll need to put your DSM codes in this section. If you do, the field where you enter the diagnosis code should be before or after this text field.

Plan

What the patient needs to do between now and the next visit and when they'll be returning.

Procedure Code

If this is a straight interview, the code will be 90791. If you do formal assessment, you'll use the applicable codes.

As for follow-ups, I was trained with the SOAP note format, so that's what I still use. It seems to be pretty ubiquitous across the medical world, so referring providers understand the format as well. There were elements of it in the initial evaluation. Here's what the letters stand for:

Subjective

This is theoretically the reported subjective experience of the client and the provider. I will generally stay with what the patient reports and leave my own impression for the assessment section. The verbs I use are typically the following: reported, stated, said, noted, described, admitted, acknowledged (those last two regarding noncompliance and the effects on treatment). I'll also comment on whether they brought completed sleep diaries, thought records, or other homework. If you had something in the plan from the evaluation or the previous session, you need to comment on whether the patient complied with it and what the result was.

Objective

Basically the same as previous objective session, your observations of the client and how they presented.

Assessment

I comment on apparent motivation and compliance with treatment recommendations and whether there's any change in the symptoms of the presenting problem. Often compliance and treatment improvement or lack thereof are connected, so I'll comment on that. I'll also describe what would benefit the patient at this point, e.g., tightening up on treatment compliance or specific things they should focus on. If they're ready to phase out of treatment or return as needed, or if they need a referral elsewhere, I'll include those things in this section as well.

Plan

Pretty much the same as previously—what do they need to do at home, and what do you plan to do next session? This is good for both you and them, especially if it's a while before you see them again.

Again, you need to include the diagnosis and procedure codes in your notes as well as the patient name and your signature. Since some people have common names, it's good to include birthdates as well, and I use chart numbers for billing so I won't have patient names in my accounting software file.

I also include session number since it's good to know where you are, especially when it comes to manualized treatments like cognitive-behavioral therapy, which have expectations of pacing and length. I also like to give my screening measures to my insomnia patients every five visits so we can track progress with more than just sleep diaries. Additionally, I note the patient's times in and out since they'll determine what your procedure code is and are good to have documented in case of insurance audits and whether someone else was present, either a trainee observing or the client's spouse or parent. I don't do family or couples' therapy, so if you do, you still need to notate who was in the session but be sure to use the appropriate procedure code.

Sometimes I need to do a treatment summary, either during treatment if someone is requesting information about the patient, and the patient wants me to release information about their treatment to someone who is not directly involved in their care, or at the end of treatment. The information included in these treatment summaries are:

> Patient name, birthdate
> Number of sessions
> Dates seen
> Presenting problem and when they presented
> Course of treatment and treatment response. You can include applicable social, medical, and psychiatric history here as well.
> Further recommendations and/or treatment plan
> Diagnosis code
> Signature

While it can be tempting to wax poetic or lengthy in your notes, reports, and summaries, I encourage you to keep them short, both for the ease of your own future review and to help referring providers, who don't want to read a novel on every patient. Referral sources have complimented me on my notes, which are clear, concise, and convey the necessary information. The secret is templates.

As I mentioned in the EHR section, some therapists feel constrained by templates, and I do use them less for my general psychotherapy patients, at least when it comes to the subjective section. However, they're a nice way to make sure you cover everything and to keep your process efficient. Some providers prefer to use a psychotherapy notes template and then transfer the pertinent information into the official note. That's fine, but make sure your psychotherapy notes are clearly labeled as such and are stored in a folder separate from the rest of the record.

How do you determine what you put in a template? If you ask the same questions repeatedly, that's a good place to start. Also, if you have a fairly structured treatment program, you may find that you end up typing the same things. For example, for the cognitive component of treatment when I do formal cognitive therapy, I have the following template structure laid out:

> The thought record process was [introduced | reviewed], and the patient worked through [an example | examples] on the [first | second | third | fourth] thought record. The patient's thought record was reviewed, and [cognitive distortions | key questions | rational responses] were introduced and applied.

The double brackets end up being drop-down menus in my EHR, so you can see that rather than typing the sentence, I choose which of the two sentences I want to use, pick the applicable option from each drop-down field, and delete what I don't use. Some EHR systems aren't quite so fancy with drop-down options, but at the very least you can put in the sentences and then fill in the fields. Either way, you're cutting down on your typing and allowing yourself more time to spend with your clients and/or actually get other stuff done between sessions. Since the availability and features of EHR systems change frequently, I don't recommend any in particular. This is one place where it's useful for you to speak with others in the field or put out a question on a list-serv.

Other documents that you may benefit from having templates of include letters to attorneys or other entities requesting records. My office manager has these and will do the letter for me to review and sign, but if you don't have an office manager, having something available keeps you from having to reinvent the document for each request. She also has a template for patient closing letters.

If you're looking for specific examples, I recommend Zuckerman & Kolmes (2017) *The Paper Office for the Digital Age: Forms, Guidelines, and Resources to Make Your Practice Work Ethically, Legally, and Profitably*. This book also comes with a CD-ROM with templates. Remember—templates are your friends. As I mentioned previously Dr. Rebecca Beaton also has resources for sale at http://www.drbeckybeaton.com/shopping-center.html.

Paperwork for Contact with Clients

What are closing letters? Since we need to ensure we keep up with our clients, it's good to touch base with the ones who haven't been in for a while for both ethical and financial reasons. Due to the fact that for private insurance, you need to file a claim within 90 days of the date of service, we send out closing letters to patients who haven't been in for two months. This allows us to catch the rare claim that hasn't been filed before it's too late and to follow up on ones that haven't been paid for other reasons. From a clinical perspective, the closing letters will nudge clients who said they would call for an appointment but haven't been back in touch. When I finish with a patient, I'll tell them to expect a closing letter. Some patients remember that I told them and some don't, but generally the letters do what they're supposed to do. Of course, you want to be careful with your wording, but people will still make their own interpretations. For example, I got a call from one anxious patient who had received a closing letter and wanted to get in touch with us before we "expunged" them from our records. I don't say anything about removing people from our records in the closing letters, but it goes to show that no matter how hard you try, clients will sometimes misinterpret what you say.

As part of our ethics code, we do need to offer to refer clients elsewhere for services if they decide to discontinue with us but still need care. There's a common misconception that we need to provide them with at least three names. There is actually no rule about the number of referrals you provide. It's also important to let clients know that we usually don't know what insurances other mental health providers take. If someone wants to see a different provider and wants to use their insurance, I'll invite them to look at their insurance website, find providers who look like they might be a good fit, and I can let them know if I'm familiar with any of them. This is also how I'll often refer to psychiatrists.

Whenever a client contacts you, that contact needs to become part of the chart. Before I had an EHR, I had a telephone contact note, but that got tedious. My current EHR has an area for comments, which is where I'll write a brief summary of the telephone call. I won't do this for questions about when appointments are or scheduling. For those, I'll make a note on the bottom of the message slip, which is placed in the paper file. If there's a clinical question, I'm sure to note it as a comment.

Since correspondence with patients is included in the file, and email exchanges can get unwieldy, I actively discourage my patients from emailing me except in very special cases, such as if they're having sleep problems while traveling overseas. This is why it's good to have a clear email policy. I'll will remind patients of this policy when I send them sound files for the exercises we do in session, remind them that email is not a secure form of communication, and encourage them to call the office with clinical or scheduling questions. This is both for confidentiality and since I may see an email, acknowledge it in my head, and then think I've answered it because I've thought about it. No, I don't multitask well.

One possible solution to the email quandary is to have an EHR system with a patient portal. Many clients have already been somewhat trained to use this type of system by their physicians' offices. This allows you to set aside time to check the portal and answer messages, which corrals the interference and ensures you don't miss anything in the shuffle of the rest of your electronic correspondence. It also means the messages become part of the patient record automatically.

Some therapists encourage their clients to email them. This is both a personal and a professional decision determined by how accessible you want to be between sessions.

Telemental Health

Health care accessibility, especially mental health care, continues to be a hot topic in the field. Rural areas have often been viewed as a challenge for therapists because being in a small, tight-knit community increases the risk for dual relationships, but people in that area may not have the time or resources to drive into a city. In my part of the country, the Southeast, there's still a lot of farmland and undeveloped wooded areas, and for some potential clients, the nearest major city may be several hours away. Some people are willing to make the trip or will stack their doctor's appointments to have several in one day. I've had patients drive to Atlanta from Alabama, North Carolina, South Carolina, and Tennessee, and I've considered, now that I've been licensed for ten years, seeing about reciprocal licensure in the bordering states.

I'm going to put a caveat here that this is one of those areas that is changing constantly, and by the time this book is out, the rules may be different. If this is an area you want to keep up to date on, check out the Telemental Health Institute at telehealth.org.

One of the primary ethical challenges to telemental health is that the provider has to be licensed in the state where the client is located when they're talking to you, or the *originating site*. For example, I'm licensed in Georgia, so if a client wants to do therapy with me while they're located in Alabama, I technically can't. If you're filing Medicare, the client's location needs to be in an area that has been designated as having a shortage of mental health providers or a county that doesn't include a "Metropolitan Statistical Area," or urban center (Department of Health and Human Services, 2015). There's a website where you can see whether your client qualifies (https://datawarehouse.hrsa.gov/tools/analyzers/geo/Telehealth.aspx). In my case, when I took Medicare, there were plenty of areas in Georgia that were several hours away. These communities are particularly in need of both physical and mental health care with the closing of several local hospitals over the past few years. Even if a community has a therapist, they may not have the training or specialty that some clients need.

The advent of the internet has allowed me to offer services to people all over the state without them having to drive several hours to see me. I will typically require people to come in for one or two sessions so we can get a sense of each other before switching to online treatment. Some clients prefer to continue face-to-face, which is fine, but I make sure they are aware of the option. I've also used telemental health sessions when a patient has been experiencing too much anxiety or has thrown their back out and can't make it in but still wants to talk. As you can imagine, this has therapeutic implications, and I don't want to enable avoidance, so this is a rare occurrence.

Is telemental health weird? That depends. If you've ever done a Facetime or Skype call with someone, it's very similar. No, the old phone session is no longer allowed. Medicare, surprisingly, has been the leader in defining what's allowed for telemental health along with the Veterans Administration. They require that you can both see and hear the client and that the interaction is occurring in real time. Since so much of what we perceive about our patients in session is nonverbal, this makes sense. As mentioned above, Medicare does put a lot of restrictions on the use of telemedicine, so before you try it with a Medicare patient, I encourage you to read through the materials.

There are other ethical considerations to follow. First, since you and your client will be discussing protected health information, the platform you use has to be encrypted and secure, and ideally the company that hosts the platform will sign a Business Associate Agreement. Many therapists use Skype, but that's not secure, and they won't sign a BAA. You also need to ensure the internet connection itself is secure. Wireless networks can be hacked, so I prefer a wired connection. It also seems to be faster and more reliable than wireless. There are several options for platforms, so research them, find out which features you need, and determine which works best for you. I also suggest you try a few to make sure they work as you need them to. Most of them will give you a trial before you have to start paying.

Second, you have to consider the possibility that the patient may require emergency services. It's much easier to hospitalize someone when they're sitting in your office. Therefore, you need to confirm the patient's physical location at the beginning of every session.

Third, when you have patients do homework between sessions, they need to be able to send things to you. For example, I use sleep diaries in my work, and often thought records. Patients have the option of faxing these to me, which is theoretically secure since it goes through the phone line, or emailing them, which is not. I explain the security limitations to them, and it's in my paperwork, but most opt to email their sleep diaries in. Some telemedicine platforms may include a secure file transfer feature.

As for billing, use the same codes you would otherwise, but with the modifier GT. Some insurance companies will reimburse for telemental health sessions, but others will not. I always suggest my patients call their insurance companies first to make sure the services will be covered, and if not, I'll switch them to self-pay or sliding scale. Documentation is the same plus a comment at the beginning of the note that this is a telemental health session on _____ platform, and the client's physical location was confirmed as _____ address. Most of my telemental health patients call in from home, but one does from work and home.

There is a lot of good additional information on telemental health in Box 8.1.

Conclusion

As you can see from the chapter and the interview, the world of therapy is constantly changing, and sometimes the ethics code takes a while to catch up. Whatever you do, document as much as is reasonable, particularly if you're making a decision about a gray area. Also remember that you have resources available through your state licensing board and malpractice insurance carrier.

Now I'm going to shift focus slightly to an area related to ethics but often neglected—therapist self-care.

Box 8.1: Interview with the Expert: Eric Marine

I had the pleasure of speaking to Eric Marine, Vice President of Claims and Risk Management for American Professional Agency, Inc. He gave me the opportunity to ask the questions that I hear come up repeatedly in ethics continuing education courses. This is a long interview, but I felt he explained these topics better than I could (E. Marine, personal communication, January 5, 2017). It has been edited for length.

First, could you define risk management for my readers?

Risk is a rather broad term. What it encompasses is chance of loss, opportunity to get into trouble and management, and figuring out ways and strategies to avoid it or minimize it.

What is the most common thing for which psychologists and other mental health professionals get in legal trouble?

That's a complicated question. The highest volume of problems rises out of family work. Not because the psychologist does anything wrong, but because they're generally involved in a conflict to begin with, especially if they're treating children. The general reason for treating children is because the parents are in conflict, and if they're in conflict, they tend to want you to choose sides. If you don't choose their side, you're obviously on the other party's side.

Psychologists also do an awful lot of work for courts, and therefore if they do an evaluation of somebody for custody of something, one of two parties isn't going to like it or maybe neither party is going to like it. Now they're basically protected from having any legal action taken against them because of the court community, but it doesn't stop a complaint to the licensing board, which is basically where everything goes even though they're groundless, and almost all of them are dismissed. It's still a way of getting back at the psychologist for "not doing what I want."

What is the best way for a psychologist to protect themselves from something like this happening?

Basically, keep good notes. Be detailed. Be thorough. Follow the approved APA or state guidelines for doing something. Again, you're talking about people in conflict, so there really isn't any way you can stop them from acting out. What you can do is minimize the possibility it will damage you in some way.

Again, almost all risk management in mental health goes back to keeping good notes. I've listened to many practitioners over the years talk about the fact that they only keep minimal notes because they're trying to protect their patient. If you understand what notes are, you understand it's a record of the treatment you're providing. The more complete the record, the less likely that it will be misunderstood. I'm kind of a stickler about that.

So if a complaint does go to the licensing board, what should the psychologist do?

Get in touch with their insurance carrier because most policies for psychologists have some coverage depending upon what level you purchase for having legal assistance with a board complaint. And the first thing to do is to activate that. It's not a penalty. And the reason it was put into coverage, 20 years ago I guess, was because prior to that, psychologists being conflict avoidant, would generally, in order to avoid a problem with the board and maintain their license, sign what's called a consent agreement saying, "I promise, I won't do this again." The problem with that is it gives legal credence to any claim being brought against you because you've already admitted you had done something wrong, which creates a bit of an issue. Therefore, the insurance industry will tell you that we can't really fight something that you've already admitted to.

When do we have to surrender our records? And what's the best thing to do when we get a records request?

Understand that you're the custodian of the patient's record. The records are released at their request. You do not release them, the patient does. Therefore, when you get a release, you comply with the release. Now there are conditions, and depending on the state, there may be some other nuances to it, but I'm speaking in general terms. That's the only time you would release records unless you receive a court order. Court order trumps everything.

Now a subpoena requires compliance up to the point where it causes you to break the law. Therefore, if you get a subpoena for records—now this is in most states—you have to respond to the subpoena, but the response can be, "I'm sorry, I don't have a release." But it cannot be ignored because if you ignore it then it starts getting into all kinds of other problems. But as far as a release of records is concerned, it's always controlled by the patient. The only time that it may not be directly controlled by the patient is if you're on the panel with an insurance company. And if you're on the panel you agree to let them audit your records, and the person who's insured by that company has generally agreed to let the audit occur when they bought the policy. So that's about the only time it's outside that circle.

What are some areas of risk management that maybe you don't see a lot of people getting in trouble for, but that mental health practitioners tend to miss?

Sometimes, because of the relationships that are developed in therapy, objectivity is lost. It's just basically sometimes people forget what their job is, not intentionally. I find most practitioners in the mental health field to be quite altruistic. But that altruism sometimes leads to naiveté. The other thing with mental health practitioners is, as I said, they're conflict-avoidant. Therefore, they're easy to pick on because they're not going to fight back because that's not the nature of the business that you're in. I'm thinking in terms of the most expensive type of claim, which is a suicide. The causes of a claim for suicide very rarely have to do with the treatment provided. It usually has to do with survivor guilt and trying to transfer the guilt to somebody. And again, the mental health professional basically is passive. And your own professions—I don't know how to put this nicely—if I put five psychologists in a room, I got eleven opinions.

And so therefore, in hindsight, everybody's got 20-20 vision as opposed to the person who's dealing with the problem immediately. And, when a claim is made against a professional, it's made by expert opinion. As I said, I can get an honest opinion from almost anybody that's diametrically opposed to the treatment that was provided, and that creates a bit of a problem. That's why documentation is absolutely critical.

What would you consider to be minimum requirements for good records?

The records requirements for the state of New York [AB note: where he's located and does programs] are if you died tomorrow could somebody look at your chart and start working with the patient from that point?

Because there are no real rules. It's been a year since I've been in touch with the academic community, but I don't think it's taught in college, as to how to take appropriate records. One of the things that's coming along is the Electronic Medical Records (EMR)... it's drop down and you have to hit all the boxes. You can't just ignore stuff. So I think that's going to help in terms of the type of records that are supposed to be kept. But, again, it's also that the younger generation is more electronic savvy as opposed to the older generation, which was paper and pencil. So, I tend to think it's going to work itself out. But, again, this has been the biggest problem.

What would be an ethical way for a psychologist to get reviews?

Mention it to your patients. Just don't make it a requirement. But, I mean, the fact that you say, "Look, I'm on Google and if you'd like, and we've had a good thing, if you'd like to write up a little piece for me, I'd really appreciate it." But just don't make it a requirement.

There is an ethics standard that says that we are not to solicit testimonials from our patients, so that doesn't fall under what you suggest for reviews?

I get questions about this all the time. And that is the ethics and practices of the profession are progressing, or evolving, slower than the technology and the usage of the population. Because you can do it, should you? Favorite question, or not favorite question, but common question, my patient's moving to Missouri and they don't want to give up our relationship. Is it okay if I Skype with them? And the answer is no.

Why? You don't have a license in Missouri. Okay? Second of all, isn't it good for you to support them with their life decision? Since they're making a change, shouldn't you be supporting that change? And, oh, yeah, just because you can do it doesn't mean you should and I'm not naive. I know people are doing it, believe me. But, again, we've got something now that people are trying to use the internet for expanded practice, in some instances, for providing service where none exists. But, again, the ethics, the license, the code of conduct, the ethical practice standards haven't been developed for it and they're not moving very quickly...

But, again, the fact that you can do it doesn't mean you should because there's all kinds of things that aren't going to happen. I mean, little known things, or little thought of things, are like, you realize that your license is a revenue stream for your state, which in your case is Georgia. All people that are licensed now have to send in their check every year or every two years. It's revenue.

Second of all is a consumer protection issue, in that your state regulates the practice of psychology in order to allow the public to be secure in the services they receive. So in order to call yourself a psychologist, you must have a license or work for a university in the state in which you're doing it. You may have your PhD or Psy.D., but you're not a psychologist in any state where you don't have a license.

That's just one of the regulatory hurdles, the multi-state license. You've got to get 50 different countries to agree on something. Plus, you're also poaching potential customers for other psychologists if you come into a state where people are trying to make a living.

Do you like or support any of the current telemental platforms?

They need to sign a business associate agreement or have the availability of a business associate agreement. There are secure platforms out there. I don't recommend any of them because, again, it's not my place and I'm not really a video expert. I just know of them and I tell people the things to look for. Make sure you've got a secure platform that has a 256-bit encryption system, that is HIPPA compliant, and is willing to give you a business associate agreement.

Is there anything else that you would like readers who are looking at starting up their private practice to know or to focus on?

The big thing is record keeping. The other thing I would recommend people do is develop a relationship with a lawyer locally so that you can talk to them. You don't need to necessarily have them on retainer, but you can talk to them for 15 minutes and it's not going to cost you too much. But they know what's going on and they're able to direct you in your practice.

Number two, realize you're a psychologist. That means you're smart, but you don't know every field. So when you need a specialist like an accountant, or a lawyer, you get one. Because most people going into private practice don't. And that's where they start making mistakes.

You need to talk with people. You need to network. The other thing I would recommend, for all of you, is develop a professional will. You don't know when you're going to die or when you're going to become incapacitated. Your family is not supposed to look at your charts. So how are you going to deal with that issue?

What should be in a professional will, then? Who you leave your records to?

What I've recommended to people over the years is to develop a group that you all guys agree to look out for each other should something catastrophic happen. Now that doesn't mean you take over the patients, but somebody with a license can go through the chart. Because they're bound by confidentiality. And, they can go through the patient record and call them up and say, "Oh, by the way, Joe Smith died." Because they're licensed and they're professional. And if he'd need a referral, they can give them a referral. But, again, you don't know if you're going to get hit by a car tomorrow.

Bibliography

American Psychological Association (2017). Ethical Principles of Psychologists and Code of Conduct Including 2010 and 2016 Amendments. Retrieved from http://www.apa.org/ethics/code/.

Department of Health and Human Services Centers for Medicare & Medicaid Services. (2015). Telehealth services: Rural health series [downloadable pdf]. Retrieved from https://www.cms.gov/Outreach-and-Education/Medicare-Learning-Network-MLN/MLNProducts/downloads/TelehealthSrvcsfctsht.pdf.

Zuckerman, E.L., & Kolmes, K.K. (2017). *The paper office for the digital age: Forms, guidelines, and resources to make your practice work ethically, legally, and profitably.* New York: Guilford Press.

You—The Most Important Care Target

9

Sometimes in private practice, engaging in self-care can feel difficult. You're an entrepreneur, provider, office manager, and marketer, so when do you take time for you, and what do you let slip when you do? While it can be tempting to put yourself last, remember that the most important business asset you have, beyond referral sources, office equipment, or even clinical expertise is YOU. Therefore, caring for your well-being is taking care of the health of the business, and you're ensuring that you preserve the quality of the care you give your patients.

How many times do we tell our clients that if they don't take care of themselves, they won't be able to effectively care for anyone else? If you end up burning out, there may not be anyone to take your place, especially if you're in a very specific niche. Sadly, provider suicide is a reality because many of us who go into the field are deeply sensitive and caring people, and sometimes providers are drawn to care for those who have problems similar to theirs. Dealing with psychological problems can be a lifelong process, and stress can often make our anxiety/depression/eating disorder/OCD emerge in a new and more virulent form.

Even if you don't struggle with mental health challenges, sometimes life gives us nasty surprises. No one is immune to grief, whether it's over the loss of a person, a relationship, a community if you've moved, or some measure of financial security. Or, more recently, the loss of a certain idealistic worldview and the exposure of some hurtful and hateful elements of society.

I have often wished that being a psychotherapist guaranteed a peaceful and drama-free life and family, but that's not how the world works. I've experienced several losses of different kinds over the past few years. One that hit me the hardest was the death of my beloved tuxedo cat, Bailey, in 2014, both because he was my favorite cat and because his passing came on top of several other losses. I know I'm not the only therapist who has struggled with the death of a pet. Sometimes we feel the loss of a beloved animal companion more than we do the death of a family member because we interact with our pets daily, and when they're gone, it changes the home environment. When we've been engaged in—or trying to engage in—Rogers' unconditional positive regard, our animals, who give us unconditional love without asking much in return, can be our greatest comfort.

All that said, if you've built a practice structure that allows for balance and self-care, you'll be better able to manage the crises that happen as part of life. There are several good books on self-care and burnout prevention for therapists, so I'm going to give you the practices I've found most useful and encourage you to read further. Resources are listed in the Resources and References appendix. Also, remember that relaxation techniques and Mindfulness aren't just for our patients. Sometimes it can even be helpful to discuss with our clients how these techniques have helped us. For example, I will do the Body Scan as part of my mental routine when I get in bed, and I've shared that with my clients, who have been more likely to try it—and benefit from it—as a result.

Like with therapeutic strategies, you can find inspiration for self-care routines and principles in Mindfulness. Let's talk about some mindful principles and how you can use them yourself. Who knows? You may find something to inspire or further connect with your clients as you engage in caring for yourself.

Self-Care Strategy Number One— Managing the Present

At this point as you're planning out your practice, you may have an idea of what it will look like, how busy you'll be, and what your days will contain. Or you'll really want to know what's coming up. When I started my practice, I would obsessively look at the calendar and see how many patients I had in a day and week, both at the end of one week and then in the morning. While it's good to be prepared for your caseload, it's not good to put too much energy into it because schedules change. There's a cliché that therapist's kids end up being screwed up, and I suspect that's because we use a lot of emotional energy on the job and sometimes may not have enough left over for family and friends.

That's the first lesson—budget your energy and recognize it will fluctuate, but that it will work out. I've had times when I've had cancellations for various reasons, leaving several holes in my schedule. At first I would freak out and lament—I'm not going to make my minimum number, I'm going to go broke, I'll fail. Yes, the fear of failure is strong with my psyche. I blame my overachiever personality. Eventually I came to realize that on weeks with lots of cancellations, I had other obligations. Maybe edits came back for a book I was working on, or it turned out I came down with a cold or some other physical challenge that made frequent rest periods a necessity. At this point with two careers, there's no such thing as an idle hour. While I don't know that I'd recommend a second career for everyone, I do appreciate being able to have the flexibility in one to give time to the other.

That's also one of the beauties of private practice—you don't have a set number of hours you have to be there, so if you have a quiet day, you can go home or run errands if you like. It took me a while before I stopped feeling like I was playing hooky when I would do so. At this point, if the first or last patient of the day cancels, or if I get a long lunch, I'm excited because it's easier to get other things done with longer chunks of time. The most exhausting kind of day for me is one where I have a client every other hour because I have to switch my focus so many times.

At this point, I'm able to manage my energy because I've had abundant opportunities to practice and lessons learned from failure. Whenever I become sick, it forces me to evaluate whether I've been pushing myself too hard and if I need to make changes, not necessarily in my schedule, but in how I approach it. Having trainees has made me remember that it takes time to build therapeutic stamina, so that's something I encourage you to think about as well. Maybe you're building your practice after hours while working a day job that's heavy on clinical work. If that's the case, you're either already in great therapist shape or on your way to burning out already. I typically start my trainees off slowly, just a couple of days a week at first, so they can build up their concentration and emotional management skills. These are things to continue to work on. Even now I find myself exhausted at the end of a busy client week, whereas at the end of a week of more paperwork or administrative tasks, I don't feel nearly as tired even though the hours worked are the same.

Another way to manage the present is to figure out how to let work stay at work. Our job puts us into contact with many sad stories and tragic situations, and being empathic humans, the effects of those tales can linger with us even after session. The first thing to do is to give yourself credit for doing what you can for these clients and monitor your thoughts to ensure you're not engaging in should statements or otherwise struggling with situations you can't control. If you have a spiritual practice, you can pray for your patients or imagine sending them light and positive energy at the end of the day and/or during your spiritual practice time.

The second self-care strategy to help maintain life/work boundaries is to have a ritual, whether it's a few minutes of meditation or something else to help you let go of your day. When I first started my practice, I had a 25 (on a good day) minute commute, and if traffic was clear, I'd take the interstate home. I would imagine going backwards through my day and leaving my patients one by one on the overpasses I went under with their energy detaching and fluttering away behind me like a gray streamer. I did tell one patient about this one, and they came back with a big smile and told me they imagined throwing their difficult coworkers off overpasses to let go of their day. Not exactly what I was going for, but hey, whatever works.

My third tip for this section is to schedule breaks. In my first practice situation, I scheduled a lunch hour for myself, but I was the only one at first to do so. Some of my colleagues would work twelve to thirteen hour days without a pause aside from the ten to fifteen minutes between sessions. One of them would heat up her lunch around noon and then run to the break room throughout the afternoon and take a few bites whenever she got the chance. The weird thing is that they were in private practice, so no one was forcing them to work through meals. After I got there, one of my colleagues, who is about my age, started scheduling a lunch for herself and said it made a huge difference in her stress level.

The bottom line is—when you're at work, be at work. When you're at home, be at home. When you relax, relax from everything. What do I mean by that? When I told my husband that I was writing the section on self-care, he said, "Oh, you mean things you should do but don't?" Yeah, he's snarky like that. I asked him what he meant, and he said something about me working on books on the weekend rather than truly taking time off. That made me think about my personality style and how I hear my clients say they have trouble relaxing.

If you have difficulty being still and non-productive, I encourage something I call productive relaxation. If you're an achievement or results-oriented person, then maybe rather than sitting and watching television—which I don't find relaxing unless I'm really tired—find a hobby that allows you to learn about and make things. Or jump on the adult coloring book craze, or something else a little more active and results-oriented as long as you enjoy the process as well as the result. I do consider reading to be a perfectly acceptable activity, probably because it has varying levels of mental activity. I split my reading time between fiction and nonfiction books that are research for my fiction, which engage my mind. Just be careful—if a hobby becomes a second career, it may bring in the same kind of pressure that your primary career does, which defeats the purpose. Right now I have this book, which is my deadline book, and a fiction book that's not promised to a publisher, so it's my fun project. I'm taking my time with it, doing research on Asia Minor, and essentially playing and reveling in the learning process.

Another thing to be careful of is perfectionism. Some clients have told me that coloring makes them anxious because they're worried they'll use the wrong color or not stay in the lines. How's that for diagnostic? Whatever you choose for a hobby or for active relaxation, allow yourself to not be perfect. For a while I was taking exercise dance classes with my best friend. While I enjoyed trying to improve, I also loved that it didn't matter whether I did everything perfectly. I wasn't performing, just having fun.

One colleague, the one who started taking lunch after she saw I did, had already planned her schedule, so she didn't have to work every day of the week. It's important to plan out time to address non-revenue-generating tasks like dealing with insurance or other paperwork. At this point, I work three full days and one half day per week with the afternoon of that half day being set aside for supervising my post-doc and the seemingly random paperwork that can pile up otherwise. It's also a good time for me to do business tasks like monitoring the budget, balancing bank statements, and ordering supplies. As for my full day away from the office, I sometimes end up going in, but I try to keep it for writing and appointments. It can be hard to figure out when to see a doctor when you're one yourself, but it is necessary.

Self-Care Strategy Number Two—
Managing Expectations

We've all had the experience of dreading an appointment, whether it's one of our own or one someone has with us. But how often does it end up being as bad as we anticipated? It's usually not, and as I tell my patients, I've wasted a good worry. Those anticipations are the mind's way of trying to control and prepare for the situation, but letting go of them will be good for managing your stress.

Another expectation to work on is how to manage cancellations, both internally and with your clients. Internally, you can't take them personally even if they feel like rejections. There will be times when you feel like you've got great rapport with a person, they seem motivated for treatment, and then they cancel their second or third appointment and don't want to reschedule. At this point, it's good to employ a shrug and an "oh, well" and move on. Sure, you might think about the session or sessions and figure out where things went awry, especially if this scenario happens repeatedly. But sometimes it's going to happen, and you can't take it personally. For example, I had one patient a few years ago who came for one session and then disappeared. I thought the initial evaluation had gone well and wracked my brain for what I could have done wrong. As it turned out, nothing. They recently called for an appointment, came in, and said they just weren't ready yet at that time but are now very motivated.

Regarding cancellation policies, this is a good place to practice modeling setting limits. My policies clearly state that if someone doesn't show up or cancels within 24 hours, they're taking a spot from someone who needs it. As one of my patients who had their own business said, "Oh, it's an opportunity cost." I understand that life happens, so I do something a little different and have a tiered policy. The first cancellation is $50. The second is what I would've gotten from their insurance company for the appointment, or, for self-pay patients, $100. The third cancellation and beyond are $150, and if someone cancels three times in a row—late or not—they need to speak to me before we schedule them again. At that point, it's disruptive to the schedule, and they may not be ready for treatment. New patients also get three times to try to come in, but if they cancel or no-show that first appointment three times, they won't be seen in the clinic. This is both for the sake of the schedule and because it's an indicator they won't be able to commit to the follow-up schedule required by the kind of treatment I do. It also indicates they're not ready to make therapy a priority for themselves, so how likely are they to do the homework?

Sometimes someone will come in, seem to be compliant, and still not improve. Or they'll come in, be noncompliant, but still want to come see you. Ethically we're not supposed to keep someone in therapy if we're not benefiting them, but dismissing a client—or "firing" them, as the terminology goes—can feel like a failure on our part. If you take nothing else from this section, remember and repeat—you can't help everyone. And you don't have to. Yes, you want to help whoever comes to you, but sometimes circumstances beyond your control are in play, and you won't be able to. Or maybe it's just not the right time for them. I have had clients who didn't do well with their first round of CBT-I but who came back a year or two later, tried again, and did beautifully.

Sometimes our hyper-responsible minds can end up wanting us to take the entire blame for a client not working out or for treatment having failed. With therapy outcomes depending as much on what the client does—at least in the cognitive-behavioral world—as what the provider tries to implement, a lot of it's out of our control. I have a file in my drawer with cards and notes of appreciation from clients for whom treatment has been successful, and when I'm feeling discouraged, I pull it out or look at some of the small tokens my patients have given me. Those can lift my spirits and remind me that I am an effective therapist.

Not having to keep patients you're not helping or don't fit well with is another benefit of being in private practice. Whereas psychologists in agencies or medical systems don't have the luxury of being able to refer out, we do, and that's freeing because it allows us to budget our energy for people we're actually able to help. This doesn't mean we can refer out clients we don't like unless they're coming for long-term therapy, and if you do so, you have to be very careful about it. If someone's coming for short-term, structured treatment and you're the only provider in the area who does it, you may have to suck it up and see them. However, if it's still not working out, you can mutually agree that they can seek help elsewhere.

Self-Care Strategy Number Three—Awareness

Have you ever had a day at work when it's the last place you want to be? Or a time when getting up and going to the office seems an insurmountable obstacle? Or you've noticed a feeling of anxiety when you're driving in?

Now add in feeling impatient with what your clients are telling you and wondering why you're even doing this. There will be times of struggle when you encounter such emotions and reluctance, but we do have to be aware of another possibility—burnout.

Burnout is a term that has been given many definitions, but the common thread is that of not having enough resources in your emotional well for either yourself or your patients. In their book *Leaving It at the Office: A Guide to Psychotherapist Self-Care*, which I recommend, Norcross and Guy (2007) use the term emotional depletion and go on to elaborate, "when the emotional drain from work-related factors is so great that it hinders personal and professional functioning, the therapist is likely suffering from burnout" (p. 56). In their book, *The Resilient Practitioner: Burnout and Compassion Fatigue Prevention and Self-Care Strategies for the Helping Professions*, Thomas Skovholt and Michelle Trotter-Mathison go further with their definition of burnout as "profound weariness and hemorrhaging of the self" (p. 103). They identify seven factors that contribute to burnout and seven areas of prevention, which I've turned into this chapter's worksheet. Since you're currently setting up your practice, you have a great opportunity to structure it to minimize the possibility of burnout.

Norcross and Guy (2007) make several excellent points in their book, but I'm going to focus on the ones that have made the most sense for me.

First, remember how I talked about having productive hobbies for relaxation? They agree and note that doing something with a tangible, visible result can help with the frustration that can come from the sometimes ambiguous nature of psychotherapy. Not seeing outcomes isn't so much an issue for me with my time-limited CBT and CBT-I patients, but it can be when I've got someone who started with me for insomnia and decided to continue with me to manage a chronic problem such as depression. These authors also encourage introspection to figure out what may be more relaxing and balancing. I'm a strong introvert, so for me quiet time is perfect. One of my dietitian colleagues is a strong extravert, so I suspect he's either energized by the work or relaxes by engaging non-client others at the end of the day.

Handling burnout is also a good area to practice self-compassion. If you do end up feeling burned out, don't judge yourself. We're all going to have problems with it at some points. The important thing is to recognize it and rectify it before it affects the quality of your clinical work. If it's part of your career and practice journey, you're not alone. Sometimes circumstances are going to pile up on you, and it might be a signal that it's time to make a change.

One term I've heard repeatedly recently is "compassion fatigue." Skovholt and Trotter-Mathison (2016) define it as occurring "when one hears the telling of the Other's story as traumatic or when the chronicity or severity of client/student/patient suffering over time is great" (p. 111). Vicarious trauma is similar, but occurs in the short-term. Think about the heaviness implied with the term fatigue. I've experienced that feeling, where it feels like I'm exhausted to the core of my being. If that occurs, it's definitely time to make a change or take a break.

One strategy for avoiding burnout that most of the authors I looked at agreed on was taking time away from your practice. I talked about managing the present with short breaks above, but of course you need to plan out longer breaks in your year. When I figure my budget, I try to plan for what amounts to a week off each quarter in addition to holidays everyone gets like Thanksgiving. This gives me the flexibility to get away and also to fit in conferences, which I attach to vacations so I can write off my travel expenses. Since I'm losing income during time off, I'll sometimes work on that half or full day I would normally not see patients the weeks before and after.

I often don't take time off during the first quarter unless it's a couple of days around my birthday or my husband's, which are close together. This gives me a buffer for more time later in the year. The fourth quarter can be especially tough with regard to cash flow, but I've learned to go with it. I usually take the days before and after Thanksgiving and the weeks between Christmas and New Year's off since I learned early on that no one comes in during that time. One year I had an 80 percent cancellation rate for the two days I worked during that week, so I decided never again. That week off positions me to feel refreshed and ready to tackle the practice again.

When is the best time to take a vacation? It seems that after a couple of years, it would be possible to track patient flow and see when the slow times occur so you can plan your vacations accordingly. I've tried that, and it seemed to work for a while, but the past few years have been weird aside from the times I've already mentioned. I've checked this with other allied health providers, and they've agreed—typically slow times have been busy, and some typically busy times have been less so. Plus, once you get established enough, there's always someone who wants an appointment during a certain time. I've also learned to work on federal and state holidays since those employees like to come in on their days off. Try to look across several years before you determine ideal vacation time. If you're starting out, think about your community. I've noticed that around local school start and end times as well as breaks, more people cancel. I also have fewer patients during the times when the nearby university is off, although that could be an opposite pattern for faculty and staff, who may have more availability when school isn't in session.

Vacations are an area where I've learned to set strict limits around email correspondence. If someone calls the office, my administrator will let me know if they're in high distress, but otherwise saves the message for when I get back so it won't disturb my time away. Emails aren't so easy to avoid. Even if you have an away responder set, you still get the emails. Consequently, I've had to talk to a couple of my patients and request that they not email me when I'm away. When I frame it in terms of my self-care, they typically understand. This is where it's helpful to have a patient portal as part of your EHR.

One area of awareness it's impossible to avoid is that sometimes people will come in with problems that highlight things that you're struggling with in your personal life. Several clients have expressed disappointment that my life isn't perfect, and I have to admit I agree with them. I don't self-disclose inappropriately, so I don't tell them if I'm going through something similar to what they're experiencing unless it's pertinent to the discussion. I tend to agree with the Acceptance and Commitment Therapy perspective that I'm more of a guide than an authority, and I'm on my own journey while they go on theirs. That said, if something gets to be too much, either because I'm facing it with a client or for other reasons, I seek my own therapy. It can be really hard to escape that expectation of "healer, heal thyself," but it's okay to admit that we can't.

Oh, and then there are regular illnesses. I admit, I've come to work with a cold if I feel I'm well enough it will not impact my clinical work. Stomach bugs are a definite stay-at-home situation. I've also come to the conclusion that if I come down with a certain severity of upper respiratory illness, it's best to just cancel the day and stay at home. That keeps me from exposing my patients to it and helps me get through it faster since I'm resting and not pushing myself. Yes, it's lost revenue, but it's also ethically responsible to not make your clients feel worse by giving them a physical illness on top of their psychological distress.

Finally, no matter how careful we are to structure our practices to avoid actively suicidal clients—unless that's your area of interest, in which case I fully support you—we're going to encounter patients who are skirting that self-destructive line. The first time I did, I wasn't prepared for the visceral physiological reaction I had afterward, like I'd been shaken to my core even though everything worked out okay. At this point, having a specific self-care strategy for such occasions is especially important because it's too easy to turn to unhealthy coping mechanisms like drinking too much alcohol.

Conclusion

As mental health practitioners, we often end up holding ourselves to high expectations. Sometimes we can get seduced into the mindset that we need to save or at least help everyone who asks for it regardless of the cost to ourselves. The take-home message from this chapter is that we are just as worthy of care as our clients, perhaps more so since we carry their burdens as well as our own. Just as we need to keep our automobiles tuned up, we require regular downtime, exercise, sleep, good nutrition, and other maintenance to perform at optimally effective levels. We also need to not fear asking for support, whether it's from our spouses, partners, friends, or colleagues. Remember—you're worth it.

Bibliography

Norcross, J.D., & Guy, J.D. (2007). *Leaving it at the office: A guide to psychotherapist self-care.* New York: Guilford Press.

Skovholt, T.M. & Trotter-Mathison, M. (2016). *The resilient practitioner: Burnout and compassion fatigue prevention and self-care strategies for the helping professions.* New York: Routledge.

Worksheet 1—Signs of Burnout

Since you're starting out, you may not need this worksheet immediately, but go ahead and look through it and make note of areas you think you may have trouble with. We all have personality-driven and learning-driven vulnerabilities. For example, I know I'm a perfectionist, and I tend to take on more work than I should. Those can lead me to overcommit and then feel badly when I struggle to meet my obligations.

I've based the questions below off the burnout factors discussed in Skovholt and Trotter-Mathison's 2016 book *The Resilient Practitioner: Burnout and Compassion Fatigue Prevention and Self-Care Strategies for the Helping Professions*: "work overload, lack of control, insufficient reward, breakdown of community, unfairness, significant values conflict, lack of fit between the person and job" (from Table 6.2, p. 106).

Is my current workload too much for me? Do I feel I can keep up with this level of commitment and activity for the long-term? Is my body telling me it's becoming exhausted? Am I not able to schedule sufficient time for activities that will keep me healthy (e.g., eating nutritiously, exercise, sleep)?

1. Do I feel that I've lost control over my schedule? Can I choose what I do and don't do? At this point, am I running my practice, or is my practice running me? Do I have specific self-care routines in place?

2. Do I feel that I am being fairly compensated for my work? Have I been accepting too many sliding scale or reduced rate patients? Am I paying myself a fair salary?

3. How often do I speak with other professionals in my field? Do I have someone I can reach out to with questions? When was the last time I met with another mental health practitioner face-to-face for an enjoyable event? Do I need to make more effort to connect with others who can relate to what I do?

4. Do I feel I am being treated fairly by my clients or by the insurance panels I'm on? Is it time to update my policies to set better boundaries? Or do I need to change my policies so I'm being fairer to my clients? Is it time to look at my insurance situation and see what panels I can drop? Or, if I'm self-pay only, has my overhead increased to the point I need to raise my rates?

5. If I look at my mission statement, do I feel that I am still practicing according to my values? Have the demands of business put me in conflict with my values? For example, have I become too focused on chasing money, and am I not spending enough time in altruistic or pro bono work?

6. Is private practice still right for me? Am I sacrificing too much personally to sustain this? What changes do I need to make to help the practice fit me again? Or is it time to do something in addition to, or different from, what I'm doing now?

Worksheet 2—Self-Care Checklist

Timing

- I will take _____ week(s) off per year/quarter in addition to holidays to refresh and rejuvenate myself.
- I will take _____ minutes in the middle of the day for lunch and to catch up on office tasks.
- I will aim for _____ patient appointments per week, preserving _____ half-days for administrative and paperwork time.

Boundaries

- I will say on my outgoing voicemail message that I will return calls within _____ business day(s).
- If I have a light client load, I will focus on tasks such as _____, _____, and _____, realizing that business will ebb and flow.
- My after-hours arrangement will include:

Self-Care for the Mental Health Practitioner

- After being exposed to the high stress of dealing with a suicidal client, whether I have to involuntarily commit them or not, I will decompress and relax by: _____
- Especially if I am in solo private practice, I will keep up in a social way with my colleagues and aim to have lunch, coffee, or happy hour with one of them _____ time(s) per month.
- After a full client day, I give myself permission to not do anything beyond what is necessary at the end of the day.

Self-Care, General

- I will exercise _____ times per week.
- I will aim to get at least 7-8+ hours of sleep per night (no, you don't get to fill in that blank unless you're a confirmed short sleeper).

- I will spend at least _____ hours/week with family, friends, and/or spouse to help me maintain my perspective as a human, not just a mental health practitioner.
- I will engage in _____ (non-therapy related hobby) at least once per week.
- I will give myself permission to just "veg out" and relax _____ evening(s) per week.
- I will engage in _____ (spiritual or Mindfulness practice) to maintain my own internal equilibrium.

Business Growth and Other Income Streams

Growing Your Business   **10**

One thing I've come to learn about business is that growth means bringing home more money over time. If you're going to bring home more money, you need to increase that "bottom line," or profit. As I mentioned earlier, there are two ways to do so—increase what you're bringing in or decrease what you're spending.

There are different types of income. You're already familiar with one kind, which is what comes in as a direct result of your effort. That's the patient or client income you bring in by treating people and being paid for your services. A few years ago, I started hearing the term "passive income." At first, it sounded like cheating, as if someone was making money they didn't work for. Then I found out the true definition—income that comes in without you having to be directly involved with it. For example, my book revenue is passive income. I work really hard writing the material at first, but once the books are released, I don't have to do much for them aside from occasional publicity.

One of the more popular ways to develop a passive income stream is to have people work for you. Then you get a portion of what they bring in, either through taking a percentage of what they're paid or by taking all of it and paying them hourly or with a salary.

This chapter is primarily for those who have an entrepreneurial spirit to the point that they want to grow their practice, and parts will apply to those who may not want to expand but do have a passion for training. One of the unfortunate aspects of business is that the more people you involve in whatever capacity, the more complicated it becomes, and the more work you create for yourself. In this chapter, I'll attempt to share lessons I've learned about employees and trainees so you can make an informed decision about your own practice in the long run.

Timing Growth and Finding Employees

As I mentioned in the section about practice names, it's necessary to consider from the beginning whether you want to grow your practice. Even if you don't make that decision right away, it's good to leave room for the possibility. For example, when you look for office space, consider finding one that you can afford and that will allow you to expand, perhaps with a storage or break room you can convert into a provider office if needed.

How do you know when it's time to bring on another provider? When your schedule gets full to the point that it's difficult to get people in for follow-up in a timely manner, even when running a cancellation list, that's one sign. Another would be if you can't get a new patient in for several weeks. It can be tempting to want to keep all the referrals to yourself, but if people have to wait, especially if there are other therapists in your areas who do what you do, they'll likely be lost referrals anyway. In *Seeing the Big Picture*, Kevin Cope (2012) asserts that businesses need to plan to grow because if they don't, their competitors will swallow up their market. I don't see private practice as being quite so cutthroat—I've known plenty of providers who have done just fine for decades as solo practitioners—but it is something to consider. I prefer to think of it from an abundance perspective, as Dr. Rebecca Beaton teaches in her business workshops. There are plenty of people who need our help, so there's enough business for everyone. So why not hire people to see those clients under your umbrella so you can benefit financially from it?

There are several ways to find people who may be a good fit for your practice, and if you're serious about growing your practice, this is one area where you need to be persistent. I might tarnish my image as an expert here, but that's okay—you're reading this in part to learn from my struggles. It's possible that you won't find someone perfect on the first try. Or, second. Or, third. Here's what happened to me.

I found my first contractor through word-of-mouth. They had approached a colleague at Emory about training in CBT-I, and he referred the person to me. After talking, we found we had mutual interests, and they agreed to join my practice. They read the contract and signed immediately. First red flag—don't trust the decision-making abilities of someone who signs a contract without careful consideration. They then went home, thought about it, and wanted to come back and amend the contract. I don't remember what they requested, only that I was irked that they hadn't taken the contract seriously enough the first time. I amended the contract, and then they came back after a two-week vacation—yes, right after theoretically starting with me—and wanted to amend the contract again. At that point, they admitted they just wanted the training so they could use it as a stepping stone to their own health coaching practice. We ended up voiding the contract, and I sent them on their way. Meanwhile, they'd gotten access to all my materials. At least their flakiness carried on. The last I heard, they'd pulled something similarly flighty in another state.

So that was the first one. Lessons learned—insist that they carefully read the contract and consider it before signing, and make expectations clear that I'm looking to build my own practice, not be a stepping stone to someone else's.

The second contractor came to me through a mention I put out on a list-serv. I got very rudely and unprofessionally called out in front of the entire list-serv by the moderator for putting a job posting on an email list—they wanted us to pay to list jobs and office space, which I wasn't aware of—so I dropped out of that organization but was happy that the information had gotten passed along. That particular provider ended up being very good clinically but had some health issues that prevented her from staying with the practice. She did have the contract reviewed by a lawyer, who actually made some good suggestions. The problem was that when you bring on a contractor, due to the time and resources they take to train and house as they're getting their caseload going, the practice loses money on them. Plus, since I was now responsible for another clinician, I wanted to ensure that we were fully in compliance with federal HIPAA and HITECH regulations, so I had invested in an EHR at the recommendation of my compliance people. It ended up being a pretty costly investment that I would have otherwise delayed. The fact that she didn't even last a year made for a financial burden for the practice and me personally. It kept me from being able to attend a friend's wedding in England. I couldn't be too resentful, though, considering she had it much worse with her health issues, and I knew she would've stayed if she could.

Lessons learned—put an early termination clause in the contract, and sometimes crap just happens, so don't make large financial investments until you're sure someone is going to work out.

I had a couple of trainees, who I'll talk about in a future section, before bringing on my third contractor. This one came to me through word-of-mouth. I had known her graduate advisor for several years, and he mentioned he had a student who would be moving to Atlanta and who would be looking for a job. She sent her resume, which looked good, and I talked to her while she was on her post-doc and then officially interviewed her once she had finished. She was already trained in behavioral sleep medicine and seemed to be a good fit for the practice, so I figured I should hire her so she wouldn't compete with me. After a year, she figured out that private practice didn't provide enough financial security, so she left for a large health system. Yep, another financial hit, and since she'd made it long enough for the referrals to build, I had a very busy first two quarters. I ended up exhausted and burned out by the time I decided to stop taking new patients for a while.

Lessons learned—be very up front about what the financial picture of joining a practice and building a caseload will look like, interview for entrepreneurial characteristics as well as clinical ones, and seriously, put that early termination clause in the contract.

One would think that after these experiences, I would be satisfied with being a solo practitioner. Nope. I licked my wounds, worked on building the bank account, and decided to do something different. A couple of things, actually. But first, let's talk about trainees.

Trainees

Once you've become established in your community, local training programs may approach you about taking on trainees. This may at first seem tempting because it would be another source of income—not the trainees paying you, but you charging clients to see them—and you may have a passion for teaching and supervision. There are a few things to consider before you do so.

First, remember that you are responsible for everything the trainees do. If they're practicum students, they require a lot of supervision, either direct observation or listening to tapes, which is time you could spend in revenue-generating activities. I have heard of practicum supervisors listening to session tapes in the car on their commute. If you're able to multitask and drive safely and give good supervision feedback while engaged in such a divided attention task, good for you. I cannot.

Another thing to be aware of is that some training programs, especially from for-profit universities, may want you to sign a contract guaranteeing a certain number of training hours. I'm all about contracts, as I'll discuss later, but you need to be cautious about what they demand of you. The number of required hours may seem low, but in private practice, there are no guarantees.

The year I had a practicum student, I signed a contract promising a certain number of hours that looked reasonable. However, several factors conspired against me. First, due to an internal change, my main referral source started not referring many of their patients, whose insurances I was out of network for, to me. Since practicum students can't see insurance patients without the in-network supervisor present in the room, that reduced the number of patients available for the practicum student to see. Also, as usual when I've brought on another provider, we ended up having the problem of patients being referred to me and not wanting to see the student. They chose to pay full fee for me rather than a sliding scale for her. Nice for my bottom line, not so great for the hours. Then after the student finally got going with a few clients of her own and sitting in with me, which meant if she did an exercise with the client she could count the hour, we had two major snow events. For those of you reading this in colder climes, that may not sound like a big deal, but do you remember the "Snowpocalypse" we had in Atlanta, where people got stuck on the roads and had to shelter with strangers because they couldn't go anywhere? That's what happens when it's sixty degrees one day, snowing the next, and the water hits the ground, melts, and freezes in the wind. We don't have just snow, we have ice, which you can't drive on, no matter how experienced you are. We also didn't have the equipment to clean it all up. So yeah, it was a mess, and the office was closed for an entire week. Then we had another snow event in February. That one wasn't so bad, but it did mean several days of the office being closed. Also around that time, I had a death in the family, which took me out of the office, so of course the student couldn't see her people then, either. As if that wasn't bad enough, I was emotionally taxed that spring with several deaths (that was the horrible spring of 2014 I referred to in the previous chapter).

To be honest, I don't like being observed in session. I'm not concerned about negative evaluation or doing something wrong. Rather, it's a drain on my mental resources having to be aware of not one, but two people in the room, and that year I was dealing with major grief on top of the financial hits to the business. Due to all the stress, both with the events of the year and with having the student in session with me, I wanted for the practicum student to finish in May, as we'd agreed upon, but she hadn't completed her hours yet. She begged me to let her continue until she finished them. I wanted to tell her no, that it was too hard on me and the practice, but I didn't want her coming after me for breach of contract. It ended up being more trouble than it was worth, and when the program asked if I would be willing to train other students, I said no. I may reconsider with a less formal arrangement in the future, especially with students from more traditional (see: not for-profit) training programs. As it was, I ended up with a six-week lower-GI bug that made me take more time off. It was miserable and showed me I had taxed my body too far.

Finally, billing for trainees can be tricky. As I mentioned, if you're going to bill insurance, you need to be present with them in session. If that's the case, there's no point to having trainees unless you're feeling like doing twice the work for the same amount of money. I typically use a very low sliding scale with them.

If you're considered to be an expert in your specialty, you may be approached by providers wanting to train with you to learn. I had one, who ended up mysteriously not working out after I asked him to sign a contract. Hmmm... The bottom line with trainees is that you have to get out of the academic mindset and consider how they fit in your business.

Communicating Expectations

Once you've been in business for a while, especially if you have an administrator or office manager who's established with you, things start to run smoothly and automatically. This is good because you don't have to think about a lot of the details relating to the office. It's also not so good because when you don't have to think about a lot of the details, you may end up not conveying them to employees or trainees. Then if they end up doing or saying something ridiculous, you have no one to blame but yourself. Sadly, people do not have the common sense one would think. They also aren't nearly as invested in your business as you are.

The best way to cover your arse with regard to making sure everyone knows what to expect is to have an employee handbook. I got my template from the QuickBooks document service, which is sadly no longer active, but you can either find employee handbook templates online or hire an HR specialist to do it. I can't promise mine is comprehensive enough to satisfy current legal requirements, but to give you an idea of what to look for, here are the things it covers:

Basic Legal Stuff

For example, this is an at-will employment state, discrimination, and harassment.

Health Requirements: Don't come to work if you're sick and can get the rest of us sick. This is also a good one for the providers to practice, as I mentioned in the Self-Care section.

Drugs, Alcohol, and Smoking: Don't do it. Also, if someone is convicted of a drug or alcohol offense, they have to report it to me.

Confidentiality: This is a very basic one and refers to the HIPAA/HITECH policies.

Violence and Safety

How to Report Injuries

Fire and Severe Weather Policies

Attendance and Punctuality: Yes, you have to define what absenteeism and tardiness mean for your practice.

Conduct

Customer Relations, Dress Code, and Appearance

Office Space Tidiness

Outside Employment and Conflicts of Interest

Payroll and Benefits Info

Acknowledgment Form: Everyone should sign this, and it should be kept in their files.

See? Most of this seems pretty obvious, but sometimes people don't think. With regard to attendance and punctuality, I didn't realize how important it was to operationalize those terms until I had one administrator—the same one who didn't realize the importance of fully sealing envelopes—who was repeatedly late and absent. It seemed obvious to me that someone should be on time consistently and shouldn't call out more than a few times per year, much less per month. I was finally able to fire her over other stuff related to neglecting her duties, but if I'd had these expectations in place, I could have gotten rid of her a lot sooner.

Rather than negligence or lack of professionalism, sometimes people just slip up, which is another reason to have everything presented in writing at the front end. One time a trainee showed up to the office wearing Capri jeans and sneakers. I sent her home with a gentle reminder that we have a business casual dress code, both in the office and while marketing. She was very apologetic, and from my previous experience with her, I knew it was an oversight on her part, not a sign of her own professional attitude.

Another area where it may be helpful to set expectations is with regard to following treatment guidelines and theoretical perspective. Again, this is something that should come with training, but some people take psychotherapy as an art further than others. It's also helpful to give trainees a clear idea of your own therapeutic perspective, both so they know what they'll be learning and so they won't expect you to supervise outside of your area of competence. For example, the practicum student I mentioned previously wanted to give one of her patients a Thematic Apperception Test, or TAT, which is a projective instrument. As you've probably gathered by now, I'm firmly rooted in the cognitive-behavioral perspective, so there was no way I was qualified to supervise that instrument. She offered to find another supervisor for that situation, but I told her no again since I'm not competent to supervise the use of that test in therapy, and I'm in the end responsible for what happens with clients in my practice. She ended up doing a different kind of assessment that I was more comfortable with.

Contracts

As I mentioned above, I had one prospective trainee who was eager to train with me until I required that he sign a contract outlining our terms. He didn't object to the financial part, but rather the noncompete agreement. He stiffened, looked offended, and said he thought we would have a "gentleman's agreement." I was tempted to look down at my non-masculine physique, then back at him, and ask, "What part of this indicates I'm a gentleman?" but I resisted the impulse and told him I would only be comfortable with everything being in writing.

With regard to contracts, it's important to have a good template, either from another practice who's vetted their contract legally, or put together by a lawyer. Since the contract is what you can go back to should any trouble arise, it's definitely worth the expense of having a lawyer look it over even if you have a template from someone you trust. Every practice is different, and so every contract will need to be tailored. Since we're not trained in legal language or procedure, we could potentially alter a contract in a way that makes that clause nonenforceable or otherwise useless to us.

I'm not going to give you a contract template since some of the applicable laws differ from state to state. For example, in Georgia noncompete clauses are enforceable, but they're not in other states. I was fortunate to inherit a contract template that I could tweak. The following is a general list of things to consider when you put together a contract or tell a lawyer what you want in one:

What the Contractor Will Do

This section indicates what services the contractor or employee will perform, what forms or paperwork are required of them and in what time frame (e.g., I have in mine that medical progress notes must be completed within two business days), how they handle termination of treatment, and that they agree to follow the ethical and procedural manuals.

Payment

How the contractor is paid, but also how client fees are collected.

Termination

What happens when the contract is over, or how the contract can be over. I'm going to consult with my attorney about adding a penalty for early termination, considering it takes two years from hiring date for a contractor to start making money for the practice after the time and expense of training and additional overhead are taken into account. It also clarifies what happens to the contractor's patients at the end of employment and a way they can work out taking their patients with them.

How Everything Fits Together and Insurance Requirements

Basically this defines who they are in relationship to the practice and also the requirement for them to have malpractice insurance and include the practice as an additional insured.

Protection of Current Practice Materials and Creation of New Ones

I have a lot of forms and handouts that are proprietary to my practice that I've spent a lot of time developing and tweaking. These sections guarantee that my materials stay with me, and if the contractor develops materials, those stay with the practice. It also protects my referral list.

Client Records

Like the forms and handouts, these remain the property of the practice.

Noncompete Clauses

This may vary from state to state as to whether you can enforce it. I signed one for my first employer before it was enforceable, which is one reason I ended up in my first private practice situation—it was outside the noncompete radius.

Advertising

The contractor can only use the business name with permission, and definitely not after their employment is terminated.

Legal Stuff

This is where it's good to have a lawyer put your contract together to ensure necessary legal clauses are in there.

Signature Page

If it's not signed, it didn't happen.

As you can see, contracts often end up being complicated because there are a lot of details. I am not a detail person, although having my own business has forced me to be more of one, so I was happy for help with this part of it. Yes, attorneys are expensive, but again, they're often worth it later. Just be very specific when you're dealing with them as to what you want them to do for you so you can minimize back-and-forth.

Taking Care of the Boss and Keeping Morale

Just as terminating with clients can feel harsh, the loss of an employee or contractor can be rough emotionally and financially. While we may try to avoid dual relationships in this area, when someone has worked for you for a while, you can become friendly and aware of what's going on in each other's lives. It's fine to connect with your contractors and employees, but it's also good to maintain barriers. The contract, manuals, and handbooks can help with office morale since having the expectations written down puts them in a space outside of you, but you're also at the end of the day going to be the one to enforce them. Go ahead and add "Human Resources manager" to your growing list of job duties.

If being a therapist can feel lonely, being a therapist and a boss can feel even more isolating in spite of having more people around you. Having employees has been one area where it's been really helpful to have advice and mentorship from practitioners who have been in the field longer. Having people who work for you can be a strange position for someone who's been trained to be exquisitely sensitive to imbalances of power, and I've found myself not acknowledging enough that I do have authority and it's sometimes necessary to remind others of that fact. There was one instance where I had been a little too friendly with one of my contractors. I was thinking about the months ahead, and I mentioned to her while we were at staff lunch one day that I'd need her to plan to be in the office during a certain week in June. That's one of the months I was on the schedule for a sleep fellow from a local training program to come observe, and I thought I was going to be out of the country for a friend's wedding. This was a good four months ahead of time, and I thought I was giving her enough notice. She went home, got mad about me telling her when to be in the office, and told me her feelings on the topic. I wasn't quite sure how to handle it, so I got some advice from a more experienced practitioner, who reminded me I was the senior psychologist, so I got first choice of vacation time, and it was okay to exercise that prerogative. It was a good reminder, and I should probably have something in the employee handbook for how vacation time is handled. This is one of those areas where it gets tricky with contractors vs. employees, though, since contractors have more freedom with their time.

Drawing boundaries around your own time becomes particularly important when you're the boss. When you bring someone on, whether they're a trainee or another clinician, they're going to have a lot of questions, especially at first. If you're in a small office, there's a possibility of them dropping in during your breaks, which may look like empty time on the shared calendar. That's fine for short questions, but even then, it could interrupt your flow, especially if you're engaged in business-related tasks that require another mindset. I also have my trainees and new hires do a lot of observation, and it took a while before I figured out I don't have to have them observe every session even if the patients give consent. Again, it's extra mental effort to be observed, even though the observers are often complimentary, and after the session it's tempting to discuss the case right away once the patient leaves. This can make you get behind on notes, though, which is annoying even if most of the notes have been done during the session. Consequently, I have the trainee write down their observations and questions, and then we set aside ten to fifteen minutes at lunch or at the end of the day for a brief discussion with the understanding that more in-depth questions can wait until the weekly supervision or peer consultation time.

Keeping in mind that lack of appreciation leads to burnout for therapists and employees, consider doing something to let the people who work for you know that you acknowledge and appreciate their hard work. I figured this one out in a previous employment situation, where there wasn't any appreciation.

I wasn't happy, and I know a lot of other people weren't either. In my practice, I've instituted monthly staff lunches, where I block off an extra hour around lunchtime and take the people who work for me out to lunch, usually somewhere local. I buy them lunch and am sure to thank them for their hard work. Sometimes they also thank me for being a good boss, which is nice. The point is more to show my gratitude for them and acknowledge that I see what they do for me.

Delegating both at home and at the office becomes more necessary the more responsibility you have. It can be difficult to move from doing everything on the front lines to stepping away and managing others. My first office manager had to remind me—gently—a few times that certain tasks were now her job. I still struggle with not doing certain things, especially when it comes to managing the appointment calendar. Having good communication is key, but so is prioritizing my time and energy for what I need to do. At this point, I've come to trust my office manager, and it helps that she's working full-time.

As for at home, sometimes after I walk in the door I feel that I cannot manage one more decision after having had intense therapeutic conversations and managing the business all day. I've had to both set limits with my husband and ask him to handle more of the household responsibilities, and then to be okay with what he decides. He manages the household budget, and I do the work finances, and overall it works out well. If you're doing everything on your own, you may need to figure out when you do your best work with both of them.

With the added stress, eating well, sleeping enough, regular exercise, and non work-related hobbies become that much more important. It's so tempting sometimes to bring work home and finish up a few things, but then you risk both the late blue light exposure that can negatively impact sleep quality and not giving yourself enough space to disengage from office stress. It may take some trial and error for you to figure out what works best for you when. For example, for me, exercise in the evening works better for me since I'm mentally exhausted, but I know people who get up really early to do it since it energizes them. Just as you advise your clients, take small steps if you need to and evaluate what's the most useful.

Other Ways of Teaming Up

Expanding your practice with providers working under you is not the only way to grow your business. Remember, there are two ways to increase profit—increasing income and decreasing expenses. Sharing overhead is one way to dramatically decrease expenses, which is why many providers go into space-sharing arrangements like I did when I first started out.

If you do team up with other mental health providers, consider the model you'll follow. Will you all treat similar types of patients and share referrals? This type of situation could get tricky because you'll end up competing with each other for both referral sources and patients. It's likely best to share space with people who do different but complementary things. Let's say you have one person who focuses on eating disorders, one who does more health psychology-related stuff, a generalist, a couples' therapist, and a child therapist. That opens up the possibility of cross referrals, and if the generalist is full and the other providers who treat adults have openings and are willing, then they can take patients who are referred to the practice. Having a "one-stop shopping" arrangement will also appeal to referral sources, who may find it easier to refer to the practice and have the office manager figure out the best placement for the client or let the client choose based on the providers' profiles on the website. In this situation, it may be helpful for everyone to be on the same insurance panels, although that's not absolutely necessary.

With "integrative health" being a buzzword and a goal in a lot of places, you may consider teaming up with other types of healthcare providers in the same practice who provide complementary services. You do have to be careful not to drive away referral sources by having the same type of provider in a space with you. For example, I've often wished I could lure a psychiatrist to join mine since I do make referrals for medication, but I need to consider whether other psychiatrists would then stop referring to me. I would have to be very clear that I would send patients back to the doctor who referred them, but sometimes patients change providers for various reasons, so that's not always a guarantee. If a client was considering changing, I would encourage them to have one final visit with the referring provider both out of professional courtesy and to give the client and the provider some sort of closure.

Also, while I do have psychiatrists who refer to me, they're not the majority of my referral sources. Who would I not team up with? I wouldn't be housed within a particular sleep clinic or sleep disorders center unless they offered me a really sweet deal, and it matched up with my business goals. I did get referrals from sleep disorders centers across the city when I started out, but now that I have competition, I probably wouldn't if I were too closely tied with a sleep clinic. That said, I am volunteer adjunct faculty in the sleep fellowship program at Emory, but I'm still in an independent practice, so that hasn't deterred other sleep doctors from referring to me.

One thing you may consider when you're looking at setting up a practice is who would help you meet your long-term goals? When I started, my dream was to have an integrative health practice with several allied health providers who focus on lifestyle changes. When I was approached by a dietitian about teaming up a couple of years ago, I was intrigued, but it wasn't the right time. I got back to him in early 2016 with the idea of sharing expenses and cross-referrals, which we already did. It's ended up being extra nice for me because as I've mentioned, I'm a strong introvert, and he's very much an extravert, so he takes the lead on scheduling and setting up marketing visits. I pay half and show up. He and I have very similar practice building goals, so the partnership has been good so far.

So who could you team up with? Think widely and outside the medical profession. Just as there's no limit with how specialized we can get, other providers also have their niches. Think about who also treats your clients. For example, if you specialize in pain, you could share space with an acupuncturist or a massage therapist who specializes in rehabilitative massage. How do you meet other allied health professionals? That's where the networking comes in.

Conclusion

I recognize that you're likely reading this book to figure out what to do to start your practice, and thinking about growing it can feel like too much. That's fine. I hope I've demystified the process for you, so you can make a preliminary decision as to whether that's something you want to do in the future. If not, that's fine. I know several people who have been solo practitioners their entire career. And this isn't a decision you need to make right away, either. Remember, that's one of the advantages of having your own practice—you can be flexible and change course later if you need to.

Bibliography

Cope, K. (2012). *Seeing the big picture: Business acumen to build your credibility, career, and company*. Austin, TX: Greenleaf Book Group Press.

Speaking and Writing 11

As you build your practice, you may find it helpful to integrate other income streams beyond those that are clinically focused. Why? No matter how interesting the clinical work, doing the same thing repeatedly can get boring. Plus, I'm guessing that many of you reading this are introverts like me, and you enjoy quiet, focused work that you can do on your own. I've had several times in my life when I wished I had chosen a profession where, as one friend said when she was in high school, "I could be locked in a room and left to work on my own." I suspect she'd been assigned too many group projects. Ironically, she just graduated with her Psy.D.

If your brain is making that record scratch sound at the thought of doing other things, take a deep breath and remember—you've already got the training. When we go through graduate school, we're exposed to more than clinical work. By the time we come out, we should have pretty good research skills and be able to put information together in interesting ways. Most of us also had teaching assistantships, and I'm guessing everyone had to do some sort of presentation, either in front of a class you were taking or a thesis or dissertation defense. The point is, we have more than just one set of skills, so we may as well use them. And as a businessperson, you may as well make money from them or leverage them to get more exposure for your practice. In his book *MBA in a Nutshell*, Dr. Milo Sobel (2010) refers to multiple income sources as one way to spread the risk. One of the nice things about having two careers is that when one is slow, I find myself able to focus more on the other.

Even beyond direct or indirect marketing, writing and speaking beyond your clinical work helps to keep your skills fresh and knowledge current. You won't give a talk without researching it first, and when you write, you may need to cite recent sources. These activities also keep your brain active with learning new things.

Speaking

When it comes to public speaking, some of you may be thinking, "No way, I can't do it. I can't get up and talk in front of a group of people." If you don't want to, that's fine, but remember—exposure techniques aren't just for clients.

The first time I got up and spoke in front of people as a businessperson, I was terrified. I was due to speak at a workshop at the Georgia Romance Writers Moonlight and Magnolia conference. This was before I had gotten my first publishing contract, and I felt like an impostor. What did I know about writing? I hadn't been successful with more than a couple of short stories. The topic was a big one to tackle, too—Personality as the Key to Internal Conflict. If you don't write fiction, internal conflict is one of those very important but very hard to nail down aspects of character development. I first did the talk for my husband and cats and timed it to make sure I had enough material, but not too much. Then I practiced with a smaller writing group, so at least I had done the talk in a lower pressure situation. By the time I got to the conference, I felt confident in my material, and it went really well. I had a full room, and people are still talking about it—in a good way.

The best part is that the experience gave me confidence going forward. At this point, I don't get nervous talking in front of people unless it's to other psychologists, and even then it's much less anxiety-provoking than previously. The more you do public speaking, the less anxious you'll be. There are also some things you can do to help yourself minimize your anxiety and make your talk as successful as it can be:

Pace Your Talk

This means to practice, obviously, and know how many slides you typically go through in a certain amount of time. I prefer to only have highlights on slides with me providing more description, so my pace is about two minutes per slide. This also helps to give you an idea where you should be at what times in your presentation. This isn't so important for shorter talks, but once you get to workshop-length, you need to keep yourself on track. It also helps to manage how quickly you go through the material and if you need to skim or skip information.

Remember That You're the Expert

The chance of you getting a question you cannot answer is very low.

If You Do Get a Difficult Question, You Can Give Yourself a Moment to Think about It

It's also okay to say those three little words—I don't know. It's very freeing to give yourself permission to say you don't know something. If you like, you can follow it up with, "But I'll look into it."

It's Also Fine to Shut Down People Who Are Talking More Than You

Say something like, "That's an interesting point, but we need to move on. We can discuss this after the talk is over." If your talk or workshop is part of a seminar or conference, you can probably tell from other talks who this is going to be. Other audience members are there to hear you and will be happy if you can control long commenters.

The Audience Wants You to Do Well

They don't want you to trip up or fail. There will usually be one or two people who have very engaged, positive expressions. Focus on them. Ignore the ones who are on their phones or who seem to be falling asleep. Also, resist the compulsion to take responsibility for a couple of sleepers. You don't know what's going on in their lives. If the majority of the room seems engaged— looking up, taking notes, nodding—you're probably doing fine.

Have Places Where You Invite Audience Participation

This is helpful in longer talks or if people do seem disengaged. In one of my sleep talks, I have a fill-in-the-blank section about sleep myths, where I put up a question like, "I should get _____ hours of sleep per night" and have people raise their hands to answer. The last time I did the talk, I gave the people who answered correctly pens. We're behavioral creatures and like rewards.

Don't Tell Mental Health Providers to Hold Their Questions

Or if you do, try to be really nice about it, although even if you do, they'll get grumpy. Yes, mental health people like to ask questions—who knew?

There are a couple of ways to get around this. Dr. Rebecca Beaton, who does phenomenal workshops here in the Atlanta area, limits people to three questions each. That cuts down on the chances of someone trying to dominate the discussion. Or you can have people hold questions until the end of a section, although I've still had complaints on evaluations when I've done that. At my next talk I'm going to give a disclaimer at the beginning that I welcome questions, but for the sake of time I may have to hold them until the end of the section to make sure the audience is getting the material they paid for.

If You Don't Want to Jump Right into a Solo Lecture or Workshop Situation, Consider Starting off with a Group Presentation, Conference Panel, or Co-Led Workshop

This sounds like the dreaded school group project, but as long as you have your expectations set up at the beginning, you should be fine. Then you can get a break while the other people are talking. Again, more people involved means more complexity, so be organized about the process.

One challenge may be in figuring out where to give talks. Remember the section on networking? All of my talks have been to organizations I'm a part of or at the invitation of someone I've met at a networking event. Most recently, I was talking to someone at a party who said she'd like to get a group of people together for a sleep workshop. Party referrals don't usually work out, at least not for clients, so I'm skeptical, but I'll follow up and see. Recall that successful networking involves you offering to help the other person. Often the individual in charge of putting together speakers for meetings and conferences is happy for a volunteer because that's one less person they need to chase down to fill a time slot.

With regard to professional organizations, the theme I've found when I've interviewed other psychologists is that generally they don't do much for us business-wise, but they're great for networking and speaking opportunities. In 2016, I gave a talk to the Georgia Psychological Association with a colleague in the spring, and I was invited to return and do an intensive three-hour workshop in the fall. The feedback was good, so I'm hoping they'll ask me to speak for them again. Sometimes psychologists in niches are reluctant to give workshops in their area because they don't want to train their competition. That's a valid point, but when you're in a niche where there aren't a lot of providers, you're going to end up with competition. I prefer to first know they know what they're doing in case I need to refer out for whatever reason. Also, I want to have contact and be able to network with people who are interested in what I do with the possibility of future collaboration. Remember that abundance mentality—there is plenty of business for everyone.

It's also helpful to think outside psychology and mental-health related organizations. It's easy to forget that people are fascinated by what we do, so if you're able to relate psychological techniques to other areas, you can pitch ideas to other professions. While other providers may not do therapy, they do engage in other face-to-face interactions where they need and want to influence behavior. For example, I spoke to a nurse practitioner group on motivational interviewing for diabetes patients about five years ago at the invitation of a colleague I'd met through the sleep world.

One thing to consider when you're putting together talks or pitching ideas is whether the material is recyclable. That talk I gave to the advanced nurse practitioners will be resurrected this summer as a workshop on motivational interviewing for the American Academy of Dental Sleep Medicine conference. Most of the material will be the same. I just need to review and tweak it.

As for practice exposure, talks are a great way to show off your skills and explain what you do, but you want to be subtle with it. I always include a slide with contact information at the end of the talk. I also have an opportunity for people to sign up for my email list. One thing I've learned recently is that you'll get more email signups if you pass around the list rather than have it to the side because people are in a hurry to leave.

So let's say you've been contacted by the organizer of a conference to come do a presentation, but you've never heard of said conference before. What should be your first step? First, check and see if the conference is legitimate. How long has it been around? Who else is speaking, or if the list isn't up yet, who spoke the previous year? Second, look and see if the attendees are paying to go. If so, your first question to the organizer should be how much they pay their speakers. Remember, the time you spend preparing for it will take time away from your practice, and your hours are now worth money. Also, many conferences are on the weekend, and I count that time as doubly valuable because it's taking away from self-care or writing. You also need to factor in travel. If you need to go somewhere, even if it's local, it will require time to get there and park. Do they reimburse expenses? Do they feed you?

One conference organizer was surprised when I asked to be paid. It made me wary of the conference and other professionals who were speaking, but I'd already stupidly committed before asking about money. I went and did the talk, and I still haven't been paid. I also didn't get any referrals from doing it, so I'll be skipping that one if I'm asked again this year.

It may be tempting to volunteer for as many exposure opportunities as you can get, but remember—people die of exposure. Not exposure therapy for public speaking, but exposure to the elements. Doing too much without compensation can sap your sense of professional worth and your time, so be careful. As for setting speaking rates, when I spoke to Dr. Michael Breus (see next section), he recommended looking at how much money I would be making at my practice for that amount of time and charging one and a half to two times that for the speaking engagement (M. Breus, personal communication, January 10, 2017). That made sense to me because I'm not only losing time for the event, but also to put together the talk.

Writing

If speaking to groups isn't for you, it's okay to focus on writing. This is another place where the internet is very helpful because there are plenty of outlets looking for content. Once you're established, journalists may contact you for an interview or quote. If you do offer to give them information, they'll typically request a quick turnaround time. They will also not run the final article by you, so be sure to be careful how you phrase things and try to avoid jargon.

One great place to find journalists looking for content is a service called HARO, or Help A Reporter Out (https://www.helpareporter.com/). It's free to sign up, and you'll get emails three times a day on weekdays with topics for articles reporters are looking to write. The topics are hyperlinked to the full request with more details and how to contact the journalist. Often the listing will say what the publication is, but sometimes they're listed as Anonymous, which may indicate it's a freelancer who's looking to pitch the article but hasn't committed it to a publication or doesn't want to reveal the publication generally.

Tips for responding to a HARO pitch, according to a freelance journalist who writes about mental health topics (and who wanted to remain anonymous), are:

1. Don't make the reporter work too hard. Include all the relevant information—name, credentials, email, website, and phone number.
2. Short bio that gives them a brief description to credit you with and shows them you're an expert in what they're asking about. You can also link to the bio on your website.
3. Two or three brief sentences responding to what they're asking for. Many HARO requests are for tips or comments. You're more likely to be quoted if they don't need to chase you down.
4. Give permission to be quoted.

5. Respond in a timely manner. The listings will have deadlines.
6. Be friendly and informal.
7. Don't be cutesy or try to bill yourself as "America's ___ expert."
8. Don't demand exposure as a condition of responding, and don't pitch your own product or website.
9. Have some sound bites on hand, so you can respond quickly.

You may notice that your local magazine, newspaper, or community website runs health articles, and you may want to approach the reporter to offer yourself as a general source. When approaching a journalist, whether freelance or for a specific publication, brevity is the key. Freelance writer Maggie Worth recommends putting together a brief email that tells the person you're available as a source, what your specialty is, where to find out more, and contact information (M. Worth, personal communication, January 6, 2017).

What do you do when someone is interested in using you as a source? Worth cautions, "Especially in your field, any press is not good press." She notes that you should consider the publication they're writing for or pitching and consider whether you want to be listed as an expert there. You should also look into the journalist and see if they've gotten any complaints or what their social media attitude is and keep notes on what you tell them in case you're misquoted. This is why I prefer to do my interviews with journalists via email—there's a written record of what I said. I like this, particularly since there's a standard in the journalism field that sources are not allowed to change quotes after they're given. Worth also noted that reporters want fresh quotes and to know if you're quoting directly from previously published material, so they can properly cite material.

As you can see, pitching to journalists gives great exposure, but may be a lot of work. I do recommend considering spending a few minutes a day doing so as you build your practice because you never know what will catch on. For example, I recently responded to a reporter from Reader's Digest. The email took ten minutes, and when she called to interview me, it took twenty more. Will I get more clients? Maybe. Does it help establish my credibility as an expert to have a *Reader's Digest* article linked from my website? Most definitely.

If you're looking for something that's a different kind of effort but with knowledge your content will get out into the world, consider blogging. As Tyra Burton, my expert in the marketing chapter, mentioned, blogging can be great for several reasons. First, it allows potential clients to get a sense of who you are and how you approach things. In the writing world, we'd say it helps them to be familiar with your "voice." Second, when you post a blog update, your website updates, which helps it in the Google rankings.

As with everything else, blog posts can take a lot of time if you're not careful. The ideal blog post length will vary, as Burton says,

> The ideal blog post length varies on your blog's purpose and posting schedule. If you are posting less frequently, maybe once or twice a month, then go for long-form blog posts that have several major points that can be highlighted in social media posts through-out the month. Long form blog posts are 1,500–2,500 words and have been getting increased social attention. One thing to consider with long blog posts is the use of quotes that are highlighted and are able to be clicked to tweet (https://clicktotweet.com/basic is one service that helps you create this). Shorter blog posts work better if you are going to post multiple times through-out the month. The more you post, the shorter each post can be, but don't forget to use some long-form content from time-to-time. With blogging it is also good to include a visual that can be used when you post links back to the post on social media. Just make sure you are following copyright laws with the images you use.
>
> (Personal communication, January 4, 2017)

For the shorter posts, I've seen one recommendation for 300–700 words. This may sound long to some. As for others, brevity may be a challenge. As Mark Twain once wrote, "I didn't have time to write a short letter, so I wrote a long one instead." As Burton mentioned, it's also important to include images for visual appeal and to break up text. Just make sure they're royalty-free. Before I started making my own writing advertising images, I got most of my stock photos and images from Wikimedia Commons. Now you can use online services like Canva to get images for $1/apiece or pay for a subscription to a stock photo site.

Let's say you have a brilliant blog post that goes viral. You may be approached by a national site for them to repost it. Here's my bias again—you're a professional, and your time is valuable, so you should be paid. Therefore, think carefully before agreeing to share your content with outlets like *Huffington Post* that make it a point of pride that they don't pay their writers.

What do you blog about? When it comes to mental health professionals, we have to be careful. While we can talk about our areas of expertise, we can't mention clients unless, as I've done in this book, we disguise identifying information to the point that they're almost made-up people. We are people, too, and remember, you sell yourself and your practice by making connections. Some judicious self-disclosure may be a good thing. For example, do you make New Year's resolutions? How do you keep yourself organized? What are your hobbies, and how do they relate to your practice, if at all?

National events and holidays may also give you the opportunity to write. For example, I did a blog post on circadian rhythms and sports performance one year after the Super Bowl. I already mentioned National Depression Screening Day. There are other mental health-related days. The internet has also given us random holidays throughout the year. The one that comes to mind at the moment is Kiss a Redhead Day, which occurs in December. Okay, maybe I won't write about that one, but I could blog about internet holidays and whether they truly connect people.

Do you read professional journals? The public is fascinated by mental health research, but aside from outlets like *Psychology Today*, there aren't many places that make it accessible. I've considered doing a little Sleep Research News column about new research and ideas that I pull from the journals I receive monthly. It would help me to remember the research, so I can talk about it with my patients.

As with giving lectures, it's permissible and encouraged to recycle content in blog posts or articles, although again, you don't necessarily want to do so with journalists. And if you do end up writing something that gets rejected in one place, figure out another way to use it. I pitched a story to *Cracked* called "Why Grandma Can't Get Therapy," in which I was going to talk about the difficulty mental health providers have meeting Medicare requirements. When one of their staff reporters contacted me, he said they weren't interested in my story (sorry, Grandma!), but rather wanted to write a story about sleep disorders, and if the editorial board accepted the pitch, I would be paid. I figured it would be good exposure, so I agreed. He asked me a bunch of questions, and I replied. And then he sent a bunch more questions, which I answered. The board rejected the story, and I ended up being out a lot of time, but I had generated some good content in an organized form that I ended up using elsewhere.

Unlike lecturing and giving workshops, which can translate into income more quickly since you presumably get paid after appearing, writing takes a little while to kick in. One important thing to remember is that it can help you create an internet presence as an expert, so when reporters from the larger outlets are looking for someone, they're more likely to find you. I've admired a colleague of mine, Shelby Harris, who is in New York and has had national media exposure for her sleep work. When I asked how she got to that point, she told me that the hospital she works with has a publicist, who she worked with in the beginning, but after her name had gotten out, the effect "snowballed."

Private practices usually don't have publicists, but if you're really interested in accelerating your media presence, you could hire one. I was fortunate to have the opportunity to speak with Dr. Michael Breus, who was one of my original sleep medicine mentors, and who now practices on the West Coast doing mostly sleep medicine. He's known nationally as a speaker and for being on Dr. Oz and The View, on which he diagnosed Rosie O'Donnell's sleep apnea, and for several sleep self-help books, most recently *The Power of When*. I'd met his publicist several years ago at a conference. Recently, when I asked him why he'd hired a publicist, he said he'd "been told to" after doing well with a guest appearance, and the show's host recommended he go for more experience and exposure. Advantages to having a publicist include having someone who already has established relationships, like the ones I've described trying to build above, and so can "leapfrog" the digital networking process. He suggested looking for local and regional publicists for those who are more focused on building a wider referral base than those who want to be seen as a national expert. The main question is: is it worth it to pay someone a monthly retainer to pitch you as an expert? More referrals from the public sphere are not guaranteed (remember what I said about direct to consumer marketing not being effective?), and he noted it's probably best for the average practitioner to stick with building an email list and reaching out to local journalists themselves. One of the main benefits, he noted, would be to have clippings of articles to include on your website or to send to potential referral sources to establish you as the local expert (M. Breus, personal communication, January 10, 2017).

Conclusion

At the beginning of setting up your practice, you may feel that you should spend most of your time settling details and taking trainings rather than giving them. At this point, I don't blame you, but I also encourage you to start figuring out a blogging schedule and get into the habit of doing so before you get too busy. You could also sign up for HARO and start looking into journalists who cover your topic area in your locality. Yes, I've spent a lot of time pursuing speaking and writing opportunities, but I've also received benefits from being invited to do more, which eventually led to paid opportunities. It's also helped me to stand out as an expert in my field and my local area, and it's always good if potential referral sources have already heard good things about you when you approach them.

Bibliography

Sobel, M. (2010). *MBA in a nutshell*. New York: McGraw-Hill.

Closing Thoughts **12**

As you can see, starting your own practice can be exhilarating and terrifying, but also rewarding. I hope this book has helped you to figure out more about your own identity as a practitioner that you can bring to your business, both with regard to the clients you help and the ways you establish yourself as an expert. In this chapter, I'm going to include some closing thoughts that will fill in some gaps and hopefully give you that last bit of encouragement to help you get started if you haven't already done so.

The Role of Professional Organizations

You may have noticed that I haven't written much about the professional organizations, but you may be wondering about whether joining them is worth it. Yes, they can be expensive, especially on the national level, and resources are tight when you're starting out. When I asked the providers I interviewed how important these organizations are for their practice, I received a wide range of responses. A third of them said some variation of, "They're not." Another third said that while our organizations can provide opportunities for networking, consultation, referrals in some specialties, the best way to benefit from them is to become involved on a leadership level. As someone who detests conference calls, I was not happy to hear this. The last third found some benefit not in leadership, but through list-servs that connect members.

Perhaps you'll agree with me that with regard to professional organizations, we as private practitioners have room to request more support, particularly with regard to business training. On a basic level, a professional organization that focuses on a specific treatment modality or disorder should have a list-serv specifically for private practitioners to request consultation with each other, or to discover other practices where they can send patients who move or who have family members who need help. And if your organization doesn't have a list like this, I encourage you to ask them to start one. We also need to be more active in making the business side of psychology more visible and accessible. Some organizations are already doing this. For example, I was recently approached by one of the organizations I belong to about doing a webinar series on private practice. I was happy to do so, but beyond that, I'd love for someone to organize a series of lectures on basic business finance.

One theme about organizations that did come up was that involvement in them can be helpful to prevent feelings of isolation for the solo private practitioner. Especially if you're in a tiny niche, it can be refreshing to talk to and get together with colleagues who speak the same clinical language you do. I found this when I was the only behavioral sleep medicine person in a group private practice. Yes, going to conferences can be expensive, but they're also useful and can be so very validating, especially if you're in an area where there's not a lot of training yet even if the treatment is manualized. I joke that I'm in the middle aged group of BSM people—and I'm totally changing that to middle tier now that I'm about to hit a big birthday ending in zero that could be considered the gateway to middle age—in that we're the ones who came along before there were formal training programs. We either had to apprentice with someone or figure out most of it ourselves. It was so nice to talk to people and have the "Oh, you do it that way, too" conversation. I will always be grateful for having this group of colleagues, most of whom are friends, that I can turn to for support and questions, and I did meet most of them through the Society of Behavioral Sleep Medicine.

Limitations of This Book

Being familiar with academic articles, you'll recall there are always limitations listed, so here are the ones I perceive in this book. I tried to give you the best information possible, but due to time constraints or other challenges, I might have fallen short in some areas. This is my attempt to be honest with you so you know what you need to investigate further.

I did my best to consult with experts in other fields and other practitioners so that you've gotten perspectives beyond my own. While I've had informal conversations with mental health providers across the country, my interviews were heavily skewed toward providers on the East Coast. I reached out through list-servs to two of the organizations I belong to, but as of the time I needed to turn the book into the publisher, I had not gotten responses to the interview questions that I had sent to the few people who responded to my query. I do feel fairly confident, though, that the advice in this book is applicable no matter where you are in the country.

Another potential bias is that I've primarily spoken with people who, like me, practice in urban and suburban areas. I would love to interview those who practice in rural parts of the country because you have a unique set of challenges with regard to maintaining confidentiality and avoiding dual relationships in places where the community is much tighter. Please contact me so we can chat for future editions of this book! Even before then, I'd love to include your perspectives on my website. Again, I do feel that most of the advice in this book is fairly universal, at least when it comes to the basics of starting your own business, no matter where you are. As I've mentioned several times, the internet has evened the field with regard to many aspects of practice.

Finally, the world is changing at a rapid pace, and there are impending challenges we can't even begin to imagine. One example that came up when I was speaking with Eric Marine, the risk management expert (see Box 8.1), is that a marijuana dispensary opened in a building in which a psychologist had established their private practice. The challenge—these dispensaries have cameras that, depending on how they're aimed, capture pictures of those who enter and leave the building. How's that for a confidentiality quandary? If you're in a state where marijuana is now legal, it's yet another thing to consider when negotiating your lease, and since landlords want to make money, they may not be so picky about who your neighbors are. I'm also finishing this manuscript at the start of 2017, and the insurance world is currently in flux. As careful as I was to give you "evergreen" information, it's possible that some of what I wrote in the insurance section may be outdated even before this book comes out.

With regard to all these areas, I'm committed to continuing to work to fill in the gaps in this information. I'll do my best to put what I find out on my own website for the book. And if you have any ideas or questions, please feel free to contact me.

Last Bits of Advice

Before I close completely, I wanted to leave you with some final advice, much of which I gathered from practitioners who were kind enough to allow me to interview them. I agree that the most important piece of advice is to be persistent because it takes time to grow a business. Those of us who go into mental health know that change takes time. So does establishing a practice.

I had a conversation with a client this morning about how the process is as important and sometimes more enjoyable than the outcome. "Embrace the journey as exciting and try to keep perspective," Julie Kolzet, PhD told me (Personal communication, November 4, 2016). I agree and love the image of "embracing the journey." When you're in the thick of trying to make sense of insurance contracts, sort out business details, and oh, yeah, see clients, it can be hard to remember that you're in a growth process. As therapists, we're in the business of growth, so it's good to acknowledge our own. When you're starting out, it may be good to sit back and give yourself credit for what you've accomplished that day, even if it's as seemingly insignificant as ordering tea for the office.

Another theme that came up is patience. "Be gentle with yourself— patience and persistence," Debra Dantzler, PhD, advised. "If something goes wrong, it's not catastrophic. Keep digging" (Personal communication, January 6, 2017). When you're dealing with a new area, it can be difficult to determine what is a major mistake and what is a minor one. Let your ethics code—and your gut—be your guide. Step back and try to take perspective before reacting. It's likely not as bad as you think it is.

Another area of frustration is how long it can take to build a strong referral stream. "Give yourself time to adjust and be patient," Katie Spencer, Psy.D., says. "Those networking 'seeds' will grow quite the flourishing practice for you" (Personal communication, January 18, 2017). One way to approach building your referrals may be to do one thing per week, whether it's reaching out to a physician's office, going to a networking event, or ordering brochures or some other fun leave-behind. Just do something. And then give yourself credit for doing it.

Finally, remember—you are not alone. Enjoy the luxury of being brand new at this and take the opportunity to seek guidance and ask questions. You don't have to be the expert, and many established practitioners are happy to help out. As Bill Herring, LCSW wrote, "Establish relationships with existing successful people in the field and find out what advice they have for you" (Personal communication, January 23, 2017).

I hope you've found my and others' advice to be helpful. If you have any questions, you can find me on my website (www.sleepyintheatl.com). I'm going to try to make this a continually developing project, so if you'd like updates and further information, please feel free to join my nonfiction and private practice newsletter (http://bit.ly/nfpracticelist).

Thank you for joining me on this journey, and I wish you much success, prosperity, and personal and professional growth!

Appendix 1

Easy-to-Search References

This is where you'll find the websites and books I've mentioned in this book. They're organized alphabetically by topic within category to make them easy to find.

Online Resources

ADA guidelines for small businesses: www.ada.gov/smbusgd.pdf

Article on therapists and social media: www.psychotherapy.net/article/psychotherapists-guide-social-media

Business structure website: www.sba.gov/starting-business/choose-your-business-structure

Form templates for sale: www.drbeckybeaton.com/shopping-center.html

IRS employee classification website: www.irs.gov/businesses/small-businesses-self-employed/independent-contractor-self-employed-or-employee

Medicare telemedicine guidelines: www.cms.gov/Outreach-and-Education/Medicare-Learning-Network-MLN/MLNProducts/downloads/TelehealthSrvcsfctsht.pdf

Website to see if a client's location is eligible for telemental health services according to Medicare: https://datawarehouse.hrsa.gov/tools/analyzers/geo/Telehealth.aspx

National Depression Screening Day info: https://mentalhealthscreening. org/programs/ndsd

NPI number website: https://nppes.cms.hhs.gov/NPPES/Welcome.do

Smart Private Practice blog and newsletter: https://blog.smartprivateprac-tice.com/

Small Business Administration: www.sba.gov/

Tax Identification Number website: www.irs.gov/Businesses/Small-Busi nesses-&-Self-Employed/Apply-for-an-Employer-Identification-Number-%28EIN%29-Online

U.S. Department of Labor Bureau of Labor Statistics: www.bls.gov/home.htm

Books

Cope, K. (2012). *Seeing the big picture: Business acumen to build your credibility, career, and company.* Austin, Texas: Greenleaf Book Group Press.

Lamb, K. (2013). *Rise of the machines: Human authors in a digital world.* United States: WANA International.

Norcross, J.D., & Guy, J.D. (2007). *Leaving it at the office: A guide to psychothera-pist self-care.* New York: Guilford Press.

Skovholt, T.M., & Trotter-Mathison, M. (2016). *The resilient practitioner: Burnout and compassion fatigue prevention and self-care strategies for the helping professions.* New York, New York: Routledge.

Sobel, M. (2010). *MBA in a nutshell.* New York: McGraw-Hill.

Zuckerman, E.L., & Kolmes, K.K. (2017). *The paper office for the digital age: Forms, guidelines, and resources to make your practice work ethically, legally, and profitably.* New York: Guilford Press.

Appendix 2

Book Resources

If you'd like to look further into the businesses owned or worked for by the experts I interviewed for the book, here they are in order of appearance:

Business Lawyer:
Linda A. Collett
The Collett Law Firm, LLC
www.collettlaw.com

Commercial Real Estate Broker:
Weslee Knapp
Keller Knapp Realty
www.kellerknapprealty.com

Privacy and Security Expert:
Donna Grindle, CHPSE, DHPC
Kardon Compliance
info@kardoncompliance.com

Website and Social Media Expert:
Tyra Burton
Senior Lecturer
Kennesaw State University

Tax Consultant/Accountant:
Kelly Locklear
Small Business Services
www.smalbizservices.com

Bookkeeper:
Carly Berg
Above & Beyond Bookkeeping
www.bookkeepingatl.com

Risk Management Expert:
Eric Marine
Vice President of Claims and Risk Management
American Professional Agency, Inc.
www.americanprofessional.com/

This book was made so much better with input from other mental health practitioners. I encourage you to check out their websites, particularly those of Robin Day, LPC, Bill Herring, LCSW, and Joshua Spitalnick, PhD, ABPP, all of whom said that their advice to a new private practitioner is to have a good website.

Aynsley Corbett, Psy.D.
http://draynsleycorbett.com/

Debra Dantzler, PhD, LP
https://www.3dpsychotherapy.org/

Robin Day, LPC
www.robindaylpc.com

Bill Herring, LCSW
http://billherring.com/

Julie Kolzet, PhD
www.doctorkolzet.com/

Pegah Moghaddam, Psy.D.
www.livingfullytherapy.com/

Shala Nicely, LPC
www.shalanicely.com/

Katie Spencer, Psy.D.
www.bia1.com/

Josh Spitalnick, PhD, ABPP
http://spitalnick-associates.com/

Index